W9-ANG-410

Games, Ideas and Activities
for Primary Literacy

Other titles in the series

Games, Ideas and
Activities for
Primary Literacy

Second Edition

Hazel Glynne and
Amanda Snowden

PEARSON

Harlow, England • London • New York • Boston • San Francisco • Toronto • Sydney • Auckland • Singapore • Hong Kong
Tokyo • Seoul • Taipei • New Delhi • Cape Town • São Paulo • Mexico City • Madrid • Amsterdam • Munich • Paris • Milan

PEARSON EDUCATION LIMITED
Edinburgh Gate
Harlow CM20 2JE
United Kingdom
Tel: +44 (0)1279 623623
Web: www.pearson.com/uk

First published in 2010 (print)
Second edition published 2014 (print and electronic)

ISBN: 978-1-292-00095-4 (print)
       978-1-292-00107-4 (eBook)
       978-1-292-00126-5 (ePub)

British Library Cataloguing-in-Publication Data
A catalogue record for the print edition is available from the British Library

Library of Congress Cataloging-in-Publication Data
A catalog record for the print edition is available from the Library of Congress

10 9 8 7 6 5 4 3 2 1
17 16 15 14 13

Cartoon illustrations by Cathy Hughes

Print edition typeset in 8.5/12pt News Gothic BT by 30
Print edition printed in Malaysia (CTP-VP)

NOTE THAT ANY PAGE CROSS-REFERENCES REFER TO THE PRINT EDITION.

Contents

 indicates web resource available

Chapter 3 Writing 215

Generic ideas and activities

Grammar: Playing with language

About the authors

Hazel Glynne has taught for many years in a wide range of schools, in the UK, the USA and higher education, and has worked for the BBC. She is currently a literacy consultant for a local authority, which involves supporting schools and training teachers. She has published educational articles and materials and written scripts for radio.

Amanda Snowden is, first and foremost, a primary teacher, but she has been a language support teacher, a special needs advisory teacher, a director of a reading project and a primary literacy consultant. At present she works for a local authority, managing and developing family learning programmes in partnership with schools, children's centres and libraries.

Acknowledgements

Hazel and Amanda wish to thank their families and, in particular, their husbands – Michael and Mike, respectively – whose continued support has enabled this second edition to be written.

Introduction

Why this book?

The teaching of literacy permeates everything we do in our primary schools – it has no boundaries. As teachers, our aim for the children is that when they leave us to enter the next phase of their educational journey they will have a love of all aspects of literacy, combined with the requisite skills. That is to say, they are confident speakers, understand how to listen actively and attentively, can write for a range of purposes and audiences and read both books and screens for purpose and for pleasure.

To quote Kofi Annan, former Secretary General of the United Nations, 'Literacy is ... the road to human progress and the means through which every man, woman and child can realise his or her full potential.'

We have attempted in the pages that follow to offer a variety of activities, ideas and games that will go some way to meeting this ideal. Children learn when they are actively engaged. We have endeavoured to make a range of suggestions that can be incorporated with ease into your plans and both be enjoyable to teach and result in true and lasting learning.

Who is this book for?

New entrants and experienced teachers as this book can be used for those just entering the teaching profession as well as those who have been teaching for some time. You will find a combination of new ideas alongside some old favourites that may have slipped your mind.

How this book is organised

There are three chapters: 1, Speaking and Listening, 2, Reading and 3, Writing.

We recognise that the dimensions of the English curriculum are interrelated so these divisions are for purely practical purposes. Speaking and Listening are two sides of the same coin while in the Reading chapter we incorporate ideas for working with narrative, non-fiction and poetry, and in the Writing chapter ideas for a range of text types are included.

Of course, talk is the foundation of literacy. As James Britten, former Emeritus Professor of Education at the University of London, said, 'Reading and writing float on a sea of talk' (*Language and Learning*, Penguin, 1970, page 164). You'll find that many of the activities encourage purposeful talk prior to reading and writing.

What you can expect

The book can be used to aid clear planning or dipped into when you need inspiration. The physical size and layout make it straightforward to locate an appropriate activity with speed and ease.

We have suggested activities that can be used with all children in the primary school and some that are particularly useful for English as an additional language (EAL) learners.

Given the cross-curricular nature of some primary planning we have mentioned where such links can be made in a meaningful way.

Our aim has been to give you a mixture of ideas, games and activities rooted in real classroom practice. Some of these will fit neatly into your plans, meeting your objectives specifically, while others are freestanding and can be used when you have to fill the odd ten minutes – those little cracks of time – usefully and will serve to reinforce key aspects of a 'literacy-rich' teaching programme.

The second edition

In this second edition we have added a variety of activities that focus on grammar, spelling and phonics in line with the current national initiatives in the UK. The new activities are designed to reinforce these aspects in a lively and interactive way and give children the opportunity to apply their knowledge.

There is a companion website at **www.pearsoned.co.uk/glynne**. Web resources are indicated on the contents pages next to the activity title by the icon Ⓦ. Resources can be downloaded to support a range of activities. The site has been extended to include a number of games and activities that are not included in the book and which we hope you will find useful.

Chapter 1

Speaking and Listening

Generic activities and games

What's That Sound?

Developing good listening skills is vital for learning. This activity helps to develop concentration and can be carried out in spare moments during the day.

Suitable for

KS1

Aims

- To develop phonological awareness.
- To enhance concentration.

Resources

- A range of containers – plastic boxes, bags, cardboard cartons
- A range of materials that make a noise when shaken or handled – tissue paper, drawing pins and some containers, small stones, shells, musical instruments

What to do

1. This works well if the children sit in a circle. It is useful to have a familiar auditory prompt, such as a tambourine that can be shaken or tapped to gain their attention.

2. Ask the children to sit silently and close their eyes. Tell them they are going to listen for the sounds in and around the school. Sit silently for 15 to 20 seconds, then ask the children what sounds they can hear in the classroom and what sounds can be heard from elsewhere. Note their responses – the list can be referred to when you carry out the activity again.

3. Tell the class that you have some noisy materials. Ask the children to close their eyes. Ask them to identify what you are handling or shaking. For example, shake a container of drawing pins. Ask the children to listen to how different the sound is when the drawing pins are shaken in different containers and see if they can identify whether it is a metal or plastic container. How does it sound when a drawing pin is banged into a piece of wood?

4. When the children are familiar with the activity, they can be in charge and select materials that the rest of the class have to identify. This simple activity helps to develop their phonological processing ability.

Variations

- Undertake the activity in different parts of the school.
- Take the class on a 'listening walk' outside the classroom.

Telling My News

An oral recount gives children an opportunity to practise organising their thoughts. Teachers should model the activity and give the children an opportunity to prepare their task with reference to a prompt sheet. This acts as a frame for answering the questions when, who, where, what, why and how?

Suitable for

Foundation, KS1, KS2

Aims

- To develop confidence in speaking to an audience.
- To develop active listeners.
- To develop questioning skills.

Resources

- Prompt sheet (see page 8)

What to do

1. Model to the class your own recount of an everyday event with which the children can identify. Keep it simple and do not put in too many details. Try to include answers to the following questions.
   - When?
   - Who?
   - Where?
   - What?
   - Why?

Here is an example.

When?	Who?	Where?	What?	Why?
On Saturday	John and I	went to the park	to watch	my cousin play football

Other ideas include holidays, outings, a description of a room in their house, a description of an activity they attend such as Cubs or Brownies, or a recent news item. Mention that they can include a personal response which can act as a summary, such as, 'I really enjoyed the day.'

2. The children then do the same, either as a whole class or in groups or pairs (see prompt sheet on page 8). Younger children could use pictures to help them give their recounts.

3. The activity can be developed by incorporating the following prompts:

   • first

   • then

   • next

   • later

   • finally.

   Here is an example of these prompts in use.

   On Saturday I went to my friend's house. It was his birthday party and lots of other children from our class were there. When I got there everyone was playing in the garden. *First* we played on the bouncy castle and *then* some of us played football. *Next* we had a water fight, which was great fun. I got very wet but it didn't matter as it was such a hot day. *Later* we had a barbecue and ate burgers, sausages and chips. *Finally* we all sang 'Happy Birthday' and had huge slices of yummy chocolate cake. It was a great day.

Prompt sheet for Telling My News

It is useful to have lists of words available to support oral recounts.
These could be in the form of posters on the walls or cards on the tables.
Working in small groups and modelling how to start sentences with
the kinds of suggested words given below helps the children to develop
confidence and vary their vocabulary.

- **When?**
    - *At* school
    - *On* the way home
    - *During* the holidays
    - *Two* weeks ago
    - *In* the morning
    - *After* dinner
    - *Recently*
    - *The other day*

- **Where?**
    - *At* home
    - *On* the other side of the street
    - *In* town
    - *Over* the bridge
    - *Behind* the classroom

- **Who?**
    - *Me* or *My* family
    - *My* friends
    - *My* neighbours, *My* teachers

Chinese Whispers

The traditional version of this game is often played by children as a party game or in the playground. It is also known as Telephone, Broken Telephone or Gossip. It is an enjoyable activity that helps children to play with language, which is essential if children are to become effective writers. It can also be quite useful for teaching young children how to moderate the volume of their voice.

Suitable for

KS1, KS2

Aims

- To develop active listeners.
- To have fun with language.

Resources

- Some sentences on cards (optional, see page 10).

What to do

1. Initially **you** may want to start the game until the children become familiar with what they need to do. Alternatively, you can have some sample sentences written on cards that can be used by the first child (see page 10 for examples).

2. The children need to stand in a line or sit in a circle. The first child whispers a phrase or sentence to the next child.

3. Each child successively whispers what he or she believes the child said to the next child. The last child says the sentence out loud to the class.

4. If the game has been 'successful', the final sentence or message will bear little or no resemblance to the original, because of the cumulative effect of mistakes being made along the line.

5. The game has no winner – the fun comes from comparing the original and final sentences or messages.

6. Once the children are familiar with the game, you could get them to work in pairs to devise new messages.

Examples of possible sentences

- I have a small, brown, furry dog.
- I have a large, stripy, shy cat.
- My dog ate his puppy's food.
- The bike's pedal broke today.
- The park is full of people sunbathing in the summer sunshine.

Alliterative sentences, such as the following, are quite effective for this game.

- Susie skips to school except on Saturdays.
- Tina travels to the gym on Tuesdays to do trampolining.
- Grinning gerbils gobbled gigantic grapes.
- Handsome Harry hired hundreds of hippos.

Variations

- **Rumours** This is a competitive version of the game. Divide the children into two teams of equal numbers, each team sitting in a circle. A leader is chosen for each team and you then whisper a message in his or her ear. The message is passed around the circle until it reaches the leader again. You can then reveal what the original message was. The team managing to keep the message closest to the original wins.
- **What Happened?** Divide the class up into small groups. Give a verbal description to the first group of an event, such as an accident. An envoy is then sent from this group to give the information to the second group. The second group then sends a different envoy to the third group and so on until the information has been given to all the groups. The final version is then compared to the original version. This activity can be linked to work on newspaper reports.

Fortunately/Unfortunately

This popular activity – also sometimes called Good News/ Bad News – can be amusing and helps to develop focused contributions and points of view. It can be a useful precursor to written work, as well as a being a freestanding talk exercise.

Suitable for

KS2

Aims

- To develop concentration.
- To develop imagination.
- To develop speaking and listening skills.

What to do

1. The children sit in a circle.

2. Share the beginning of a story or piece of news with them, ending with the word 'fortunately'.

3. The next person continues the story or recount, but ends his or her contribution with 'unfortunately'.

4. The third person ends his or her input with 'fortunately'.

5. Continue around the circle, alternating 'fortunately' and 'unfortunately' as the last word of each participant's part of the story.

Suggestions for starter sentences

- Emma was asked to the party. Fortunately, ...
- Imran scored the first goal of the match. Unfortunately, ...
- When they arrived at the hotel, they were exhausted. Fortunately, ...
- The new school stood at the highest point of the town. Unfortunately, ...
- The news report stated that she was innocent of the charge of theft. Unfortunately, ...
- The magnificent oak tree gave shade to all those in the park at midday. Fortunately, ...
- The car sped down the road at 80 miles per hour. Unfortunately, ...
- When Aunty Jenny came to visit, she brought her pet dog with her. Fortunately, ...

Variations

- A collection of connectives could be assembled. These could be written onto cards. Each child would take a card and begin the next part of the story with that connective.
- In pairs, discuss the best and worst things that have ever happened (to you or generally).

Additional materials to support this activity can be viewed/downloaded at **www.pearsoned.co.uk/glynne**

Just a Minute

Each child is invited to talk for 'just a minute' on a topic of interest. This useful activity can be played when you have a few minutes to spare during the day, as a starter activity for literacy or as a short game to reinforce information being learned in other subject areas. It is based on the popular radio programme of the same name.

Suitable for

KS2, but can be adapted for KS1

Aims

- To develop confidence when speaking to an audience.
- To give practice in extracting the main points from a range of information on a given subject area (science, history, geography).

Resources

- Selection of topic cards (optional, see page 14 for examples)
- Clock or watch with a second hand
- A bell, whistle or rainstick

What to do

1. This activity should be modelled by the teacher initially. To begin with, it is advisable to play each round for *half* a minute instead – it is surprisingly difficult to speak fluently for a whole minute on a given topic! At first, it can be helpful to introduce the game as a paired or small group activity and only later play it with the whole class as this encourages the more reticent children.

2. Invite a child to select one of the topic cards (see page 14 for examples).

3. The aim is for the child to speak for a minute on that subject. Indicate the end of the minute by ringing the bell, blowing the whistle or turning the rainstick.

Variations

- When the children become familiar with the format of this game, you can introduce another level of challenge by asking them to speak without repetition or hesitation. If they do repeat or hesitate, they will forfeit their turn and the next child will take over.
- Organise the children into teams and ask them to challenge the opposition when there is any hesitation or repetition.
- Play a podcast of the BBC Radio 4 *Just a Minute* programme to the children as a model.
- This activity can be used to review key information taught in history, geography, science, maths and so on.

Topic suggestions

- My favourite room.
- My favourite TV programme.
- My least favourite TV programme(s).
- My journey to school.
- What I like to do in my spare time.
- My favourite holiday.
- The seaside.
- Books or comics that I've enjoyed reading.
- What I'm good at.
- What I'd like to be better at.
- My room at home.
- My favourite food.
- My least favourite food.
- Cars – my favourites.
- Fashion – what I like at the moment.
- My last birthday.
- My pets.
- My family.

Show What You Hear!

This activity focuses on developing listening skills. The children have to listen carefully to the details as a story is read to them. This could be an effective way to introduce a new text to a class.

Suitable for

KS2

Aim

• To develop active listening skills.

Resources

• A narrative text that is new to most of the class, such as the description of Mr Tumnus in *The Lion, the Witch and the Wardrobe* or descriptions of characters in *Charlie and the Chocolate Factory*
• Mini-whiteboards or paper
• Pens, pencils, felt-tips or crayons

What to do

1. Read the story to the class.
2. Select a description of a character or setting to re-read.
3. Give the children the mini-whiteboards or paper and pens or pencils. Explain that, when you read the description from the story again, you want them to draw what they think the character or setting looks like. Emphasise that this is not an exercise to judge the best drawing but instead, you want them to concentrate on the key elements of the description or setting.
4. When re-reading the passage, pause to allow time for the children to draw.

Variations

- Using the mini-whiteboards or paper and pens or pencils, this time tell the children that you're going to re-read the story but want them to draw the key events described. Allow sufficient time for them to draw.

- Ask the children to retell the story in pairs, referring to their drawings. You could label each pair 'A' and 'B' then ask 'A' to begin the retelling and at a signal, ask 'B' to take over. This can be used in humanities or science to reinforce key facts. It can also be used to introduce note taking.

Wishes and Favourites

Wishes and Favourites uses talk prompts to encourage personal responses from the children. They are particularly useful for less confident children who are reluctant to speak in class.

Suitable for

KS1 but can be adapted for KS2

Aims

- To develop more confident speakers.
- To develop active listeners.
- To encourage personal responses from children.

Resources

- A list of sentence starter prompts written on the whiteboard or cards (see page 18)

What to do

1. The children sit in a circle and you choose one of the prompts – 'My favourite food is ...', for example – and model how to complete the sentence (see box on page 18 for more examples).

2. Each child then takes a turn to complete the sentence in a different way. Initially, some children may be a little reluctant, so they could talk through their idea with a partner.

3. The activity can then be repeated using a different prompt.

Variations

- When the children are familiar with the activity it can be played in small groups and each group can have a different prompt. Over time, the children will become more confident in speaking such sentences and then the activity can be used as a precursor to oral storytelling.
- The activity can be adapted for older children in KS2 by using more challenging prompts, such as 'My hope for the future is ...', 'I want to learn to ...' and so on. Use the activity as a warm-up, either to support storytelling or non-fiction work – particularly argument and discussion.

Examples of sentence starter prompts

- My favourite food is ...
- My favourite pop/TV star is ...
- My favourite time at home is ...
- My favourite book is ...
- My favourite film is ...
- My favourite day is ...
- My favourite things to do with my friends are ...
- My favourite room is ...
- My favourite person is ...
- My favourite animal is ...
- My favourite clothes are ...
- I wish I could be ...
- I wish I could live ...
- When I grow up I wish to be ...
- I wish I could change into ...
- I wish I could find ...
- If I had three wishes ... .

Additional materials to support this activity can be viewed/downloaded at
www.pearsoned.co.uk/glynne

One for Sorrow, Two for Joy and the If Game

Here are two different activities that use talk prompts to develop children's confidence in making oral responses. These activities can be used to build children's discussion skills, but they are also useful for developing storytelling skills.

Suitable for

KS2

Aims

- To develop active listeners.
- To develop more confident speakers.
- To encourage and develop oral responses from children.

What to do

One for Sorrow, Two for Joy

1. This activity can be played with the whole class or small groups. You may want to model the activity first.

2. Each child takes a turn to complete a sentence prompt such as, 'One thing that makes me sad is ... but two things that make me happy are ...'. For example, a child might say, 'One thing that makes me sad is *a rainy day*, but two things that make me happy are *seeing rainbows and splashing in puddles.*'

3. The children can discuss their ideas with their talk partners before sharing them with the rest of the class or group.

4. Once the children have participated in the activity several times, they can begin to use their sentences as the bare bones for a story. The sentence prompts can also be adapted to support discussion

skills linked to a particular subject, such as whale hunting or keeping animals in zoos. For example, 'Some people believe that whale hunting is a good idea because ..., but I believe that ... .'

If Game

1. Initially, you may want to use the activity with the whole class as a circle game. Later, it can be used with small groups or talk partners.
2. Provide the children with a sentence prompt, such as, 'If I could fly, I would ... '.
3. The children take turns to complete the sentence (see below for more examples of prompts). It is probably easiest to start with the realistic ideas and move on to the more poetic ones when the children are familiar with the activity.

Variations

- Encourage the children to devise their own 'If ...' prompts. Unusual ones are particularly useful for developing storytelling skills or encouraging divergent thinking.
- You could use the prompts as starter lines for a class or individual poems. Some of the prompts could also be used as story starters.

Examples of prompts

- If I was Prime Minster ...
- If I could go into space ...
- If I was in charge of my school ...
- If I was an explorer ...
- If I travelled back in time ...
- If I could travel into the future ...
- If I had X-ray vision ...
- If I was invisible ...
- If I could swim to the bottom of the ocean ...
- If I could run faster than a cheetah ...
- If I was a tree ...

- If I was a raindrop ...
- If I was a ray of sunshine ...
- If I was a paper clip ...
- If I was an ant ...
- If I could read thoughts ... .

Talk Prompts for Explanation and Discussion

These activities use talk prompts to develop children's explanation and discussion skills. They are particularly useful for non-fiction work, but they can be adapted for tasks linked to fiction, too.

Suitable for

KS1, KS2

Aims

- To develop active listeners.
- To develop more confident speakers.
- To encourage and develop explanation or discussion skills.

Resources

For Because Game

- Because cards as prompts, particularly for younger children

For Plus, Minus, Interesting or Positive and Negative

- Prompt cards, with the symbols '+', '–' and '!' (for Interesting) on them if working with younger children

What to do

Because Game

1. This activity can be played in pairs or small groups. You may want to model the activity first. Ask the children to discuss an idea linked to a particular topic or subject (this could be in any curriculum area). An example linked to the science topic of solids and liquids could be 'Where does the flour mixed with warm water go?'

2. The children can discuss their ideas with their talk partners or group members before sharing them with the rest of the class.

3. As the children put forward their ideas, they use the talk prompt, saying, for example, 'I think ... because ... .' If you are using Because cards, the children can use them as a physical prompt for this sentence.

4. This is a particularly useful activity for encouraging children to explain their answers more fully.

Plus, Minus, Interesting or Positive and Negative

1. This activity can be used with pairs or small groups of three or four children. It is probably best if you model the activity first. As above, the discussion statement can be linked to non-fiction work in English or another subject area, such as maths, history, science or geography.

2. Give the children the chosen statement or question, which could be linked to an investigation or problem-solving activity, such as sorting and using materials. An example might be, 'Do we need waterproof clothes? Why?'

3. Then, allow the children five minutes to discuss the *plus (positive)*, *minus (negative)* and *interesting* aspects linked to the statement or question. You could ask the children to think of one or two ideas for each aspect.

4. The children then feed back their ideas to the rest of the class.

Variations

- When introducing the second activity to younger children, it usually works best if you focus on just one aspect rather than all three. For example, you could ask them to think of just one positive idea.
- If you want to encourage children to think more laterally you can give them a more unusual statement or question, such as, 'What would happen if you were invisible?' or 'What if all door handles were made of chocolate?'

What Am I?

This is a very well-known game and an excellent activity to use with children as it requires them to listen closely to what is said and extract the important details.

Suitable for

KS1, KS2

Aims

- To develop active listeners.
- To develop concentration.
- To develop precise use of language.

Resources

- A variety of actual objects or pictures, for example, everyday objects, two- and three-dimensional shapes, small toys (transport, wild animals, farm animals), science equipment, pictures of fruit, animals, birds, food
- A screen or bag

What to do

1. This activity can be played with the whole class or in pairs. You may want to model the activity first. It is probably best to link the activity to a theme or topic as this helps the children to focus in on the possible answers.

2. One child chooses an object or picture, but ensures that the other children cannot see it by hiding it behind the screen or inside the bag. The child then gives a clue about the object to the children and they have to see if they can guess what it is. For example, 'I am a type of fruit. I can be green or red on the outside. I am crunchy' (see page 25 for some other examples of simple clues).

3. The children can be given up to three or four clues, but, if they do not guess correctly, they are then shown the object.

4. The next child then has a turn to choose an object or picture and provide some clues.

Variations

- This activity can be made simpler or more difficult by changing the types of objects or categories used. Older children could be asked to give just one clue at a time so that the children can process the information and eliminate possible answers before being given the next clue.

- The child gives only one or two clues and then the partner or class can ask questions to help them work out the answer. This is much harder as they have to sift through the possibilities and eliminate particular ones.

- Even more difficult is to put restrictions on the clues that can be given. For example, when describing an everyday object, the child is not allowed to say how it is used. This variation is particularly good for extending children's vocabulary as they have to be quite inventive when devising clues (see below for some examples of more complex clues).

- For younger children, you can make the activity easier by having a pair of children choose an object or picture. They can then devise the clues together.

Examples of simple clues

- I am a type of vegetable. I am orange and crunchy. Rabbits like to eat me.

- I am a wild animal. I live in the jungle and roar. I have hair called a mane.

- I am kept as a pet. I am soft and furry. I drink milk.

- I am green. I live in and out of water. I can leap.

Examples of more complex clues

- *Clue* This object has handles. It usually contains a purse, keys and other small objects. *Answer* Handbag.

- *Clue* This is a small object with a thin, long handle. The other end has small bristles on it. *Answer* Toothbrush.

- *Clue* This object has a lid and a spout. It usually needs electricity to make it work. *Answer* Kettle.
- *Clue* This object is made of rubber and goes on your foot. *Answer* Wellington boot.

Who Am I?

This activity is similar to the previous activity, What Am I? (see page 24), but it focuses solely on well-known people or characters. It requires the children to listen closely to what is being said and extract the key facts or information.

Suitable for

KS1, KS2

Aims

- To develop active listeners.
- To develop concentration.
- To develop a precise use of language.

Resources

- Some pre-prepared lists or pictures of people or characters (optional, but good for younger children)

What to do

1. Play either with the whole class or in pairs. It is a good idea to model the activity before the children have a go.

2. One child thinks of a well-known person to describe. For younger children, the focus can be on characters from a class story. For older children, they can describe a famous person or someone from their current history topic.

3. The child gives a clue about the person and the class or partner then have to see if they can guess who it is. For example, he or she could say, 'I am a girl. I have yellow hair. I like eating porridge' (see page 28 for some other examples of clues).

4. The children or partner can be given up to three or four clues, but, if they do not guess correctly, the child shows or tells them who the person or character is.

5. The next child or partner then takes a turn, choosing a person or character and providing some clues.

Variations

- Once the children are familiar with this activity, instead of being given clues, they can ask questions, such as, 'Are you a man? Are you tall? Do you have brown hair?' Also, the child can only respond with 'yes' or 'no' answers. This version is harder as they have to think of questions that will give them the information they need.

- Set the children a limit for the number of questions that they can ask – no more than ten, say. Alternatively, the game can be made more competitive by, for example, making the winner the one who asks the fewest questions to get the answer.

Examples of clues for well-known characters

For Red Riding Hood

- I am a girl.
- I have a grandma.
- I wear a red cloak.

For Jack

- I am a boy.
- I am very poor.
- I planted some beans.

For Cinderella

- I am a girl.
- I am poor.
- I have a fairy godmother.

For the huntsman in Snow White

- I am one of the Queen's servants.
- I work in the forest.
- I have a hunting horn.

For the witch in Hansel and Gretel

- I am a woman.
- I live in the forest.
- You can eat my house.

Connections Game

This language game is excellent for general vocabulary work and it helps to extend children's reasoning abilities. The skill of making new connections is also an important part of the creative process. Similes, metaphors and other poetic devices are just ways of connecting two things that you would not normally associate with one another.

Suitable for

KS1, KS2

Aims

- To develop speaking and listening skills.
- To develop precise use of language.
- To extend vocabulary and promote lateral thinking.

Resources

- A collection of everyday objects or pictures cut from magazines or catalogues (see page 31)

What to do

1. Give the children a selection of the objects or pictures. It is best to give them a mixed selection in order to encourage them to think of connections that are not immediately obvious.

2. The children work in pairs or small groups and take turns to pick two objects or pictures. Ask them to explain the connection between their chosen objects. For example, 'They are both made of metal' or 'They both have handles.' The winner is the pair or group who has made connections between the most pairs of objects.

3. Once the children are familiar with the game, you can include more disparate objects as this will extend the children's reasoning skills further. For example, *paper, envelope, button, thread, needle, kite, door, vase, book, boat, saw, light bulb, iron, ladder, bottle, key, wheel, box, dog, sun, tree, aeroplane.* An example of a connection might be, 'Door and book because they can both be opened.'

4. This can then lead on to work on similes or poetry. The children can work in pairs to devise similes or poetic sentences linked to their two objects. For example, 'A book is like an open door.'

Examples of objects or pictures that can be used

Kitchen objects

Can opener, bottle opener, sieve, grater, pan, potato masher, wooden spoon, metal spoon, fork, cup, saucer, plate, jug, bowl, kettle, toaster, fridge, washing machine, cooker.

School equipment

Ballpoint pen, pencil, ruler, pencil sharpener, rubber, felt-tips, coloured pencils, scissors, glue, desk, table, chair, whiteboard.

Garden objects

Spade, fork, rake, trowel, gardening gloves, seed, flower, bush, tree, leaf, watering can, hose, lawnmower, shed, greenhouse.

Pets or farm animals

Pig, cow, sheep, dog, cat, mouse, horse, chicken, goose, duck, turkey, donkey, goat, rabbit, guinea pig, hamster, gerbil, fish, tortoise.

Zoo or wild animals

Elephant, sea lion, snake, bear, leopard, panda, zebra, tiger, crocodile, penguin, cheetah, lion, polar bear, rhinoceros, hippopotamus, monkey, gorilla, kangaroo, giraffe.

Other objects

Items of food, clothing, furniture, transport.

Additional materials to support this activity can be viewed/downloaded at www.pearsoned.co.uk/glynne

How Do You Say It?

This activity focuses on *how* we say something as the words we choose to emphasise in a sentence can change the meaning for the listener. It is a useful way to start a discussion about how we speak and how emphasis can alter meaning. It helps to raise awareness of the subtlety of language and the importance of clear delivery. It can be played with a whole class or small group, but should be modelled by the teacher initially.

Suitable for

KS2

Aims

- To develop active listening skills.
- To raise awareness that *how* we speak can alter the meaning for our listeners.
- To develop inferential skills.

Resources

- Set of starter sentences on card(s) (see page 33)

What to do

1. The first player takes a card on which is written a sentence such as, 'Jane said she'd come to the party if she could.'
2. The player reads the sentence, emphasising one word, such as 'Jane *said* she'd come to the party if she could.'
3. The card is then passed to the next player who emphasises a different word from the same sentence, perhaps saying, 'Jane said she'd come to the party *if* she could.'

4. The card is passed to the next player until all possible changes of emphasis have been exhausted. Then, another sentence is used in the same way.

Variations

- To develop the children's skills further, gestures could be added.
- A sentence could be read in the style of a particular character from fiction or a history topic.
- Change the statements into questions or exclamations.

Examples of starter sentences

The sentences can be cut up separately or all printed on one piece of card.

- John's father said he could borrow the car on this occasion if he drove carefully.
- Jo stated that she could not go to the meeting as she was feeling unwell.
- Mrs Jones agreed to go to the conference if her company agreed to pay for the ticket.
- Amit really doesn't want to go to school today.
- Emma would go to the Christmas party, but she didn't want to go to Christmas lunch.
- I didn't take the ice-cream from the fridge on Friday night.
- I decided not to buy the brown boots this month as I didn't have the money.
- I'll agree to you going to the concert if you take your cousin with you.
- Anna can come to the adventure park this time if you agree to look after her.
- James was delighted to be asked to play in the match this week against his old team.
- Kate refused to eat the apples at home, but was seen eating apple pie at school.
- 'I won't go to school', exclaimed Isobel, 'unless I can wear my new summer dress!'

Barrier Games

Barrier games are simple interactive activities. The children are not allowed to see what the other players are doing and have to speak and listen clearly to complete a task. The games help children learn how to give clear instructions and descriptions, listen well and ask questions for clarification. Children can have a physical barrier between them, such as a folded piece of stiff card or a box file. Older children can sit back to back. The games can be played between individuals, pairs or groups and the activities can be adapted to suit a range of resources, such as real objects, pictures or photographs. It may be necessary to model the games first, depending on the children's experience with barrier games.

Suitable for

KS1, KS2

Aims

- To develop use of precise vocabulary.
- To develop active listeners.
- To develop instructional language.

Resources

- Pieces of paper with a grid and shapes in each part of the grid (these could be actual, three-dimensional shapes or just two-dimensional drawings) – see page 36
- Blank grids

What to do

1. Discuss key vocabulary linked to the activity, such as the names of shapes and positional language.

2. Put the barrier up between the players and explain that no one should look at the other side of the barrier.

3. The child on one side of the barrier has the completed grid and describes to the child on the other side of the barrier which shapes to draw and where to draw them. This child draws them on to their blank grid.

4. The child with the blank grid can ask questions to clarify the information given, but they are not allowed to point or look at each other's grids.

Variations

● **Matching Pairs** The children take turns to describe an object or picture. One player describes an item until the listener locates and displays its matching pair. They repeat the process until all the items are paired.

● **Construction** One child describes the steps involved in building a particular model (using a construction kit, for example). The other child follows the instructions and tries to build an identical model.

● **Route Finding** One child describes how to get from one point on a map to a particular place. The listener draws the route on his or her copy of the map.

Note

Wrapping paper is an excellent and reasonably priced resource for barrier games. It can be used as a complete sheet or cut up into sections, for example, to play Matching Pairs.

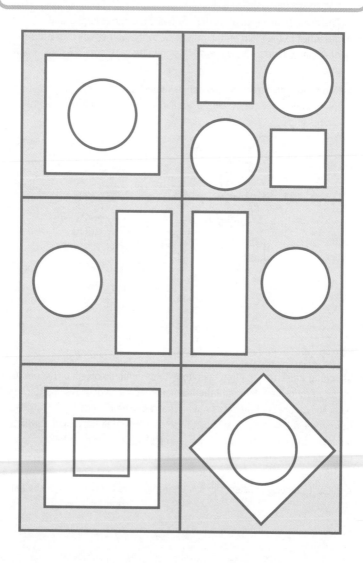

Jibber Jabber

This is a retelling activity. It can be linked to a story that the children know well, such as a traditional tale or a story that they have been studying in class. The activity can also be a way of reinforcing cross-curricular work, such as in history, science and geography. For example, the children could retell the key facts that they have found out about Mary Seacole or recap the details of a science investigation.

Suitable for

KS1, KS2

Aims

* To develop active listeners.
* To develop use of precise vocabulary.
* To reinforce or consolidate a story sequence or factual knowledge.

What to do

1. For this activity, the children work in pairs. One child should begin to retell a story or key facts (see page 38 for an example) to his or her partner. After about a minute, say 'Change!'

2. The partner now continues the story (or key facts). This pattern continues so that each child has several turns.

3. It is important that the children listen closely to each other so that they are able to continue the story sequence or key facts in a logical order.

Example of key facts linked to the history topic of Mary Seacole

- Mary Seacole was a nurse in the Crimean War. She was born in Kingston, Jamaica. Her father was Scottish and her mother Jamaican.
- She learned her nursing skills from her mother, who ran a home for wounded soldiers. Her medical approach was based on herbal remedies and good hygiene.
- Mary wanted to help look after the soldiers in the Crimea, so she travelled to England. Unfortunately, she was not taken on as a nurse so she had to pay her own fare.
- When Mary arrived in the Crimea, she set up the British Hotel and took care of the injured soldiers.
- Sadly, she is not remembered as well as Florence Nightingale, but in 1954, the Nurses Association of Jamaica named their headquarters Mary Seacole House.

Super Stuff

Using artefacts can be really helpful as prompts for purposeful talk. Teachers will be familiar with using a particular artefact, such as a marble egg, passing it around during Circle Time. When someone holds the egg, it is his or her turn to speak. Artefacts can be used during drama sessions or as part of generic (PSHE) classroom activities.

Suitable for

KS1, KS2

Aims

- To encourage purposeful talk.
- To provide a stimulus for dramatic talk and improvisation.
- To add an extra dimension to cross-curricular work.

Resources

- A range of artefacts – for generic activities, a marble egg or stone, piece of rock or jewel, plus a selection of different artefacts; for circle time, a shell (tell shell), hat (happy hat), rag (brag rag), cup (cry cup); for Topic Tins or Talk Tins, collections of artefacts relating to specific topics in history, geography, science or religious education

What to do

Generic

1. Collections of different artefacts can be used for drama games, which should be modelled first.
2. The children sit in a circle and pass around an object, miming its use. Each child should devise a different use. A wide selection of

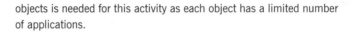

objects is needed for this activity as each object has a limited number of applications.

Circle time

1. The resources are passed around the circle of children. Each suggests a starter sentence, such as:
   - (wearing the happy hat) 'I am happy when I ...'
   - (holding the tell shell) 'I would like to tell you about ...'
   - (holding the brag rag) 'Something I'm really pleased about is ...'
   - (holding the cry cup) 'I'm really sad when ... '.

Topic Tins or Talk Tins

1. These can be used to add an extra dimension to work being undertaken in other subjects. You will be familiar with collections of artefacts for history and religious education and collections can be made for geography and science, too.

2. These artefacts can be used as a starting point for discussion and help to forge meaningful cross-curricular links. For example, a Victorian iron could lead to a scientific discussion, although the artefact might be shared initially during a history session.

Activities to support paired and group work

Talk Triangles and Listening Triangles

These are useful techniques to try once children have become experienced at talking with a partner. Working in a group of three is more difficult for them than in a pair, but it is less threatening than working in larger groups.

Suitable for

KS1, KS2

Aims

- To develop children's ability to share ideas.
- To support turn taking in discussions.

Resources

- For Talk Triangles, some cards in different colours

What to do

Talk Triangles

1. Give each group of three children three Talk Triangle cards, each a different colour from the others. As each child in turn shares his or her ideas they put their cards down on the table so that they eventually make a triangle shape.

2. When the children have given their ideas verbally, they could write down their idea on their piece of card. These could be used as prompts for the class discussion and later used as part of a class display.

3. This is a useful way to help children rehearse their thoughts. It builds children's self-confidence so that they feel more comfortable when sharing ideas with the whole class.

Listening Triangles

1. This strategy helps children to take on the roles of 'talker', 'questioner' and 'scribe' (or 'recorder'). The talker explains or comments, the questioner prompts or interviews and the scribe makes notes. The notes can be used to give feedback to the other two children or the rest of the class.

2. The children can use this strategy to prepare for character interviews or to talk through and prepare a piece of written work, such as a story. It is important that all the children are given an opportunity to experience each of the roles.

3. This is a clear and focused strategy that can also be very quick, for example, giving a talker just two minutes to explain an idea. It is also a useful way to introduce children to different roles and a valuable precursor to using the next activity, Group Roles, with children (see page 46).

Additional materials to support this activity can be viewed/downloaded at www.pearsoned.co.uk/glynne

Group Roles

Working in larger groups (of four or five children) can produce a greater range of ideas than is the case in smaller groups, but it is often useful to give each group member a different role.

Suitable for

KS2

Aims

- To develop active listeners.
- To support children's self-confidence and enable them to contribute in whole-class discussions.

Resources

- Numbered cards or labels
- Prompts for some group roles, such as observer (see page 48)

What to do

1. Before asking children to work in larger groups, it is important to establish some ground rules for talk (see page 47).

2. Divide the class into groups of four or five and give each child a number or label. If you are using numbers, link these to particular roles, such as leader, scribe, reporter, mentor or supporter, and observer. Clarify what these roles mean. Here are some examples.

   - *Leader* organises the group, encourages everyone to participate and complete a task.

   - *Scribe* makes notes about the main points of discussion and any decisions made by the group.

● *Reporter* works with the scribe to summarise the group's ideas and reports back to the class.

● *Mentor or supporter* helps the group to carry out the task and supports people along the way, explaining what is needed and so on.

● *Observer* makes notes on how a group works and shares ideas. At the end of the task, he or she shares these observations with the group (see box on page 48 for examples of prompts for this role).

3. Set the groups a task. This could be a problem-solving or investigative activity linked to any curriculum subject – maths, science, design and technology, geography, for example. Alternatively, the task could be a group discussion linked to a dilemma or a controversial topic.

4. It is important that the task is clear and tightly focused and there should be a desirable outcome, such as making a poster, model or flow chart. To ensure that the groups stay on task, there should be a time limit for the outcome. How long the children will need depends on the task, but it is probably best to give them no longer than 20–30 minutes so that they do not lose interest.

5. It is essential that the roles are changed for the next task so that the children are able to experience different ways of working within a group.

Some ground rules for talk

● Everybody has a turn to speak.
● One person speaks at a time.
● Make eye contact with the speaker.
● Speak in a clear voice.
● Be clear about what you mean.
● Respond to the other speaker.
● Make a longer contribution than just one or two words.

Example of prompts for an observer

- How well did the children work together?
- Did they follow the ground rules for talk?
- Did they find some rules easier than others?
- Which ones?

Snowballing

This is a way to share information and opinions. It develops active listening and helps children to recall main ideas and information. It is extremely useful for supporting discussion skills and can also be used to develop the children's persuasive skills.

Suitable for

KS2

Aims

- To develop active listeners.
- To support the recall of main ideas.
- To develop the skill of asking questions to clarify understanding.

What to do

1. Introduce the discussion topic – 'Is school uniform a good idea?' for example (see box on page 50 for more ideas).

2. The children form pairs and share their thoughts and opinions with their talk partners.

3. Next, each pair joins another pair of children to share these thoughts. It is best if each child shares the opinions of his or her partner as this encourages everyone to listen carefully.

4. The small groups can then join together to make a larger one, so pairs become groups of four, fours become eights and so on until the whole class has joined up. Each time, the children share their views with the new group. Initially, you may just want to move from pairs to groups of four, then the whole class until the children are familiar with the activity.

5. Once the children are back with the whole class, you can choose some individuals to explain or share their partners' opinions.

Variations

- Use Snowballing as a general technique for sharing information. So, for example, the pairs could read an extract (fiction or non-fiction) and practise explaining or summarising one aspect of what they've read. They could then get together in fours (then eights, etc.) to explain what they've learned.
- The children prepare a particular argument or point of view in relation to a topic, then they could get together in fours to try to convince or persuade each other that the argument or point of view is the right one. This could be done as preparation for a class debate in which every child is given a role.

Examples of discussion topics

- Is television a good or bad thing?
- Should you be able to buy whatever you want to with your pocket money?
- Should you be allowed to go anywhere you want to with your friends?
- Is homework a good idea?
- Is television better than books?
- Do cats make better pets than dogs?
- Should computers replace teachers?
- Should mobile phones be banned in schools?
- Is a zoo a good place to keep animals?
- Should dogs be allowed in parks?
- Should cars be banned from town centres?
- Was Jack right to steal the giant's precious things?
- Was Red Riding Hood foolish or brave to walk through the woods?
- Should Goldilocks have gone into the Three Bears' house?

Rainbowing

This is a useful group interaction strategy that develops the children's ability to share ideas and information. It involves everybody and gives them responsibility for their own learning.

Suitable for

KS2, can be adapted for KS1

Aims

- To develop the language and social skills needed for cooperation and collaboration.
- To develop the children's abilities to question and reflect.
- To reinforce and consolidate factual knowledge.

Resources

- Different coloured cards or pieces of paper, for example: yellow, orange, red, green, blue and purple

What to do

1. Divide the children into groups (preferably of equal size). These groups can then discuss a particular issue or research an aspect of a topic. For example, they could complete a science investigation linked to filtering – that is, finding out how to separate an undissolved solid from a liquid.

2. Each member of the group is given a different colour (this could be a piece of paper or card). The children then regroup according to their colours and compare their findings.

3. The activity can be completed in just one lesson, but you may need to continue over two or more sessions. This will depend on the original task given to the children and the amount of research needed.

Variations

- This strategy can be used for a variety of activities. For example, children can evaluate a particular extract or poem or they could research an element of a history topic. If they were learning about the Romans, the original groups could find out about different aspects of this topic – roads and transport, slaves, clothes, education and so on. They could then share the main points in their colour groups.

- To use this strategy with younger children (KS1), it is best to link it with the retelling of a well-known story. For example, after hearing the story of the Three Billy Goats Gruff several times, the children could be divided into groups and each group given a picture prompt (see page 53) for part of the story. Ideally, each child in the group should have a copy of the picture prompt as it will be useful later in the activity. Each group then devises a sentence to link to their picture prompt and afterwards the children go to their colour groups. The children then sequence themselves within their new groups so that they can retell the story.

Jigsawing

This is a group interaction technique that helps children to collaborate when sharing information or investigating a topic. It *can* be completed in just one lesson, but works best if continued for two or more sessions. This enables the children to research a topic in more depth.

Suitable for

KS2

Aims

- To develop active listeners.
- To extend children's ideas as they share them with others.
- To develop the language and social skills needed for cooperation and collaboration.

Resources

- Depending on the topic being researched, have available artefacts, non-fiction texts and the Internet, if appropriate

What to do

1. Organise the class into 'home' groups (preferably ones of equal size).
2. Give all the children in each home group a number – 1, 2, 3 or 4. If you have an unequal group, give two children the same number, such as 1, 2, 2, 3 or 4.
3. The children then get together in their number groups – that is, all the number 1s together and so on. These become 'expert' groups, each group being given a different aspect of a topic to investigate. For example, if the children were researching the Egyptians, the 1s could find out about farming, the 2s about houses, the 3s about food and the 4s about writing.

4. The expert groups then research their mini topic and discuss the main points that they will report back to their home groups.

5. The children then return to their home groups and each child reports back on the findings of his or her expert group.

Variation

• This is an excellent way to involve all pupils and give them responsibility for their learning. Initially it may seem a little complicated, but it works extremely well. Once the children are familiar with Jigsawing, they become adept at moving from one group to another and, at a later stage, can organise the groups themselves. It is helpful if you have an end product that is required as a result of the feedback session in the home groups, whether it be a leaflet, poster or small information booklet. This gives a focal point to the sessions and encourages the children to listen to each other's feedback.

Envoys

This is a group interaction strategy that supports the sharing of information and ideas.

Introduction

This technique is easy to organise and a useful way to maintain focus within group work. For example, if groups are losing momentum, sending an envoy can be a way to elicit more ideas or clarify their own ideas.

If you wanted to emphasise the role of the envoys, they could be given badges or coloured bands to wear. Over time, it is important to ensure that all children have an opportunity to be an envoy so that it does not become a role only particular children play.

Suitable for

KS2

Aims

- To enable children to extend their ideas.
- To support collaborative work.
- To develop the children's abilities to question and reflect.

What to do

1. The children should be organised into small groups. Once they have completed their initial investigations and discussions ask them to choose a group member to be an 'envoy'.

2. The envoy is sent to another group so that all groups have a visiting envoy. The envoys report on their 'home' groups' findings and share ideas.

3. The envoys can collect further ideas from the groups that they are visiting and then report back to their home groups.

Variations

- The envoys could be sent to do further research, such as in the library or using the Internet.
- The envoys can go to *all* the other groups, explaining and sharing ideas.

Statement Game

This activity helps to develop listening and negotiating skills. It encourages children to voice their own opinion, but also listen to others before making a final decision. It helps children to develop the ability to prioritise. The collaborative nature of the game necessitates cooperation. This activity is sometimes called Diamond Nine.

Suitable for

KS2

Aims

- To develop listening skills.
- To develop negotiating skills.
- To cooperate with peers and produce an agreed outcome.

Resources

- A selection of nine or more statement cards (see pages 59–60)

What to do

1. Choose statements that refer to topics the children have been studying in a range of curriculum areas, such as history, geography, science, personal, social and health education (PSHE). The two examples shown in the box on pages 59–60 focus on homework and school uniform.

2. The children decide whether they think the topic is a good or bad thing and arrange the cards in order of priority, as below. They can discard some of the cards.

Topics and Statements

- *Topic*
  - Homework – good or bad?

- *Statements*
  - Homework should not be given to children at primary school.
  - Homework is a good thing for children at primary school.
  - Homework reinforces work that has been covered during the day at school.
  - Homework allows parents to be involved more fully in their children's education.
  - Homework is a waste of time.
  - Homework extends the work that has been started in school.
  - Homework is fun.
  - Some homework is more useful than other homework. For example, copying out is a waste of time, but researching on the Internet is useful.
  - The teachers only give homework because they *have* to, not because they *want* to.
  - Children should be allowed free time after school to do things of their own choosing.
  - Children work hard enough during the day and should be allowed to relax after school instead of doing homework.

- *Topic*
  - School uniform – a good idea?
- *Statements*
  - School uniform makes us all equal.
  - School uniform can be expensive and not everyone can afford it.
  - School uniform is dull.
  - We lose our individuality when we wear school uniform.
  - We all look the same so no one stands out.
  - School uniform allows us to show a pride in our school.
  - Many schools in other countries do not make their students wear school uniform.
  - School uniform is old-fashioned and is not suitable for the twenty-first century – blazers, for example.
  - School uniform can be up to date.
  - Children should be involved in designing their uniform – after all they have to wear it.
  - School uniform is uncomfortable.

Six Thinking Hats

This strategy was invented by Dr Edward de Bono in the early 1980s. The method is a framework for thinking and it encourages children to communicate more effectively.

Suitable for

KS1, KS2

Aims

- To develop confidence, creative problem-solving and critical thinking skills.
- To enable children to justify and explain their ideas.
- To develop cooperation in group work.

Resources

- Coloured cards (white, red, black, yellow, green and blue) or coloured hats or PE bands
- Cards giving discussion subjects (optional)

What to do

1. Six Thinking Hats enables children to focus on separate thinking skills and ensures that new ideas are explored fully. Each hat represents a different way of thinking (see pages 62–3). The strategy is an effective one, but it is important to spend time establishing the concepts so that the children understand them. It is a good idea to introduce the hats separately – say, one per week – so that the children become familiar with each one (younger children may need a little longer). The yellow hat is probably one of the easiest to introduce and a circle time session would be a good way to begin to look at the ideas. Explain to the children that they are looking for the good points or benefits of a plan or idea. Later on, you can remind them that, when they wear the yellow hat, they are looking for positive features or how something could help them.

2. Introduce the hats alongside the vocabulary that goes with them. This can be displayed in the classroom so that you can reinforce the vocabulary on a regular basis. This is particularly important for younger children.

3. You can use the Six Thinking Hats strategy for almost any problem-solving activity, so it can be linked to a range of subjects, for example, whether they be in maths, science or geography. Once the children are familiar with the concepts, they will associate the coloured hats with key words or questions that will help to direct and sequence their thinking.

4. In a group discussion, the hats can be worn in any sequence, but usually it is best to start with blue hat thinking to establish the goals and end with blue hat thinking to summarise the ideas or outcomes. At other times, the sequence will depend on the topic. For example, if children have strong feelings about a subject it might be good to start with red hat thinking to get those emotions out of the way first.

5. Whichever sequence you choose, it is not necessary to use *all* the hats in a lesson – indeed, you may decide to focus on just one or two. It is important to remember that even once the children have learned the techniques, they will need to have these nurtured until they become part of the everyday language of the classroom. Here are some ideas for possible discussion topics.

- Should schools encourage a healthy lifestyle?
- Now that we have computers, do children still need to be taught handwriting?
- Is watching television bad for you?
- Should you be allowed to stay at home rather than go to school?
- What if people had wheels instead of feet?

The Six Thinking Hats

- *White hat*: facts and figures. This is a neutral hat that only deals with the *facts* of a situation, not emotions.
- *Red hat*: emotions and feelings. This hat expresses strong feelings, both positive and negative, about a situation. It does not have to give reasons for those feelings.

- *Yellow hat*: benefits, opportunities and hopes. This hat is positive and optimistic. It sees only the good side of a situation or idea.
- *Black hat*: problems, dangers and risks. This hat is negative and critical. It sees the bad and dangerous side of situations and ideas.
- *Green hat:* new ideas, alternatives and options. This hat produces new ideas, thinks of changes and offers new ways of seeing things.
- *Blue hat*: organising ideas, setting goals and summarising progress. This hat summarises the views of the others. It brings things to a conclusion.

Variations

- The class could use the hats to ask a visitor, such as an author, various questions.
- The hats can also be used for role play or discussing certain scenarios, such as town planners wanting to build a new supermarket on the site of the playground or the school wanting to erect two wind turbines on the school field.
- The Six Thinking Hats can also be used to support and improve reading and writing skills (see page 148 for an example linked to reading).

Storytelling

Storytelling

Telling rather than reading a story to a group of children adds an extra dimension. The audience is actively engaged in the process. Storytellers use a range of techniques to help them remember the tales. The suggestions made here help to develop both teachers and children as storytellers. A bank of memorable stories can be built up over a period of time.

Suitable for

KS1, KS2

Aims

- To develop speaking and listening skills.
- To retell a story.
- To understand story structure.

Resources

- Artefacts related to chosen story
- Large sheets of paper
- Auditory prompt (a tambourine, rainstick or bell, for example)

What to do

1. As preparation, read a short story. It's simplest to start with a familiar, traditional tale. Identify the key events of the story and the main characters. Draw a story map of the key events on a large sheet of paper and identify any artefacts specific to the story. For The Three Little Pigs, for example, the artefacts could be some straw, a stick and a brick.

2. Tell the story to the children using either the story map and/or the artefacts. They act as an aide-memoire, reminding the children of the sequence of events in the tale.

3. Divide the class into pairs, one child being 'A', the other 'B'. Pin up the story map and/or hand out smaller versions of the map.

4. The children take it in turns to retell the story to each other, referring to the story map. Each 'A' begins the retelling and, at a signal from the teacher, using the auditory prompt, each 'B' then continues (a tambourine or rainstick is useful to gain the attention of the group). Each section of the story is worked on separately.

5. This activity should be repeated several times so the story is retained in the children's long-term memory.

Variations

- Puppets, rather than artefacts, can be used to recreate the story with younger children.
- Use pictures of scenes from the story so that the children can sequence the events.

What Comes Next?

A variety of strategies can be used to begin storytelling sessions. The three given below can involve the whole class, groups or pairs and should be modelled by the teacher initially.

Suitable for

KS2

Aims

- To develop listening skills.
- To develop imagination.

What to do

Carry on the Story

1. The children sit in a circle.
2. Start off the story for about 30 seconds, ending with an open-ended connective, such as and, then, so, next, after that.
3. A child in the circle adds the next part to the story, the child next to him or her the next part and so on (see page 69 for some examples of sentences that you can use to start the ball rolling).

One-Word Story

1. The children sit in pairs, facing one another.
2. They each supply one word alternately, going backwards and forwards until they complete the story.

Finish the Story

1. Two or three of the children go out of the room.
2. They come back in, one by one, and you begin the story for each of them. They then each have to finish it. The different versions can then be compared.

Story starter suggestions

- Last week, as I was walking home from school, I noticed a £20 note lying on the ground ...
- This morning I had a real surprise. I received a letter from a TV company asking me to participate in the pilot of a new show it's trialling ...
- I am expected to go on holiday with my family and my cousin, who I really dislike. She/he always lies and gets me into trouble ...
- I have been invited to a party and I really don't want to go. I am unsure how to get out of it ...
- Many years ago, in a land far away, there lived a rich king and his three children. He knew that after his death the children would squabble over his wealth, so he decided to set them a task, and to succeed they would need to cooperate ...

Tell Me a Tale

Here is a collection of different techniques to provide children with story-making ideas. It is important that they have plenty of experience of telling stories as this will support and improve their storywriting skills. Storytellers often talk about the 'bones' of a story. The idea is that you remember just the important aspects and then you can add the 'flesh' or details. The strategies below help with this, but it is important to model all of them with the children. You could work on class versions initially before asking the children to work in pairs.

These activities were originally devised by Ben Haggarty, one of the founders of the Company of Storytellers.

Suitable for

KS1, KS2

Aims

- To develop speaking and listening skills.
- To understand story structure.
- To develop imagination.
- To retell a story.

What to do

Seven Words

1. Make a list of the seven most important words in the story, including the main characters, key objects or places. For example, *three pigs, wolf, straw, sticks, bricks, cooking pot, chimney*. This helps the children to decide what the story is really about.

Story in a Sentence

1. This is another useful way to reduce a story to its main elements, but it is probably best to it use after the Seven Words activity on page 70.

2. The children try to summarise the story in a short sentence, rather like a headline in a newspaper does. For example, 'Bad Wolf killed by Three Pigs!' or 'Cooking Pot for Huff and Puff Wolf!'

Three-minute Story

1. In pairs, the children take turns telling the story as fast as they can to their partner.

2. Signal the end of the three minutes using a cue, such as with a clap or using a bell or tambourine.

3. To reinforce the children's knowledge of the elements of a story, you can ask the listeners to check that all the important details have been included by the tellers. This ensures that the listeners play an active role, too.

Story in a Suitcase

This activity is a specific example of the Super Stuff activity on page 39. The suitcase adds a dramatic dimension as the lid is lifted to reveal a range of artefacts. A class discussion begins that may lead to dramatic activities.

Suitable for

KS1, KS2

Aims

- To develop imagination.
- To develop speaking and listening skills.

Resources

- A suitcase containing a scarf, diary, bus ticket, map, torch, foreign coins, half-written letter, addressed envelope and pair of glasses

What to do

1. Set the scene. A suitcase has been found. The owner is unknown.
2. Open the suitcase and show the range of objects inside.
3. Encourage a discussion to answer the following questions.
   - *Who* owned the suitcase?
   - *Where* was the suitcase found?
   - *Was* it owned by a man, woman or child?
   - *How* old would the owner be?
   - *Was* the suitcase abandoned? If so, why?

In this way, gradually build a picture of the suitcase's owner.

4. Alternatively, divide the children into groups and ask each group to look at one or a few of the artefacts in detail, asking and answering questions.

5. The story of the suitcase could be the beginning of an improvised drama or simply the starting point for a shared narrative. The outcome could be oral or written.

Variations

- A handbag or box can be used to hold the artefacts instead of a suitcase. These artefacts can be varied and a range of mystery stories can be devised over a period of time.

- Put into the suitcase or box some artefacts relating to a current history or science topic, encouraging the children to apply their knowledge from other curriculum areas.

- Use the poem 'The Magic Box' by Kit Wright (*Cat Among the Pigeons*, Penguin, 1989) to develop or introduce this activity.

Drama activities

Generic Drama Strategies

The notes below outline three key strategies which can be used when teaching drama to children of all ages. Each strategy can be applied to a range of activities.

Suitable for

KS1, KS2

Aim

- To experience a range of drama strategies.

What to do

Teacher in Role

1. This strategy involves the teacher participating directly in the drama. Younger children will accept this more readily than older ones. You will need to explain that you will be taking a role in the drama the first time you do so.

2. It could be useful to have a signal that denotes when you are in role. For example, you could wear a scarf or a tie when you are in role.

3. You could play a part that enables you to control the drama. For example, by being a narrator or the leader of a group.

Improvisation

1. Improvisations can be prepared or spontaneous.

2. For prepared improvisations, the group works towards creating a short play. The children learn to cooperate and negotiate and gradually refine their ideas.

3. When introducing improvisation, it is advisable to aim for a final 'play' of two to three minutes. This works well when linked to other curriculum areas, such as a history topic, when the children can directly apply their knowledge.

4. Spontaneous improvisations can be used as necessary and when the children in a class are accustomed to the strategy, which has been modelled and practised during prepared sessions.

Role Play

1. Young children readily embrace role play, often within the general classroom setting, where a dedicated role-play area is frequently located.

2. For older children, it can be useful for:

   - showing them that their ideas can be accepted and used
   - giving them practice in using a range of language
   - giving them practice in negotiating with others
   - giving them practice in dealing with problem-solving situations and making decisions
   - allowing them to adopt different attitudes.

Hot Seating

This well-known activity is very useful for exploring character and motivation. It provides practice in developing questioning techniques and, in particular, requires the use of open-ended questions.

Suitable for

KS1, KS2

Aims

- To develop questioning skills.
- To develop an understanding of character motivation.
- To develop empathy.

Resources

- A significant artefact relating to the character in the hot seat (optional, but helpful for younger children), such as a cloak, hat, crown
- A 'special' chair
- Open-ended questions (see page 79)

What to do

1. This activity works best if the children are familiar with the characters from reading a story or studying a historical figure. The strategy should be modelled by the teacher (perhaps with a teaching assistant asking the questions). Time should be given to allow the children to prepare their questions, which they might do in mixed ability pairs. They will need to devise open-ended questions (see page 79) as only eliciting 'yes' or 'no' answers limits the activity.

2. Select one child to sit in the hot seat, which is a special seat at the front of the class or group.

3. Explain that he or she takes on the role of the chosen character, either fictional or historical.

4. The rest of the class asks the child in the hot seat a range of questions. The child must answer in role.

Variations

- This can be played in pairs, each taking turns to be either the questioner or in the hot seat.
- If some children have difficulty in formulating open-ended questions, they can be given pre-set questions initially.
- Guided reading can provide a useful context for this activity. Members of the ability group could take turns at being a character from the studied story and in the hot seat.

Examples of open-ended question starters

- *How did you feel when* you acted in such a selfish/kindly way?
- *If you were to be in that situation again,* how might you behave?
- *Why do you always act in* such an arrogant/thoughtful/harsh/careful way?
- *Who would you choose to accompany you* on a similar adventure/ outing/event and why?
- *How did you feel when you* were betrayed/let down/succeeded in winning?
- *What do you plan to do next and why?*

Remind the children of the key words: who?, when?, where?, how?, what?, why?, might, could, should. These could be written on cards or the faces of a cube. The 'why' and 'how' questions promote open-ended answers. Adding 'should', 'could' or 'might' to the question words adds a further dimension. For example, the children could ask:

- *'What would* happen if ...?'
- *'Who might* appear ...?'
- *'When could* something occur and why?'

Thought Tracking

This activity is helpful when exploring character. Each child takes on the role of a character and explicitly articulates their thoughts. This technique helps children to get 'under the skin' of a character and can assist when discussing motivation and how a character might feel at a particular point in time.

Suitable for

KS1, KS2

Aims

- To analyse a character's thoughts, feelings and motives.
- To look at the difference between what characters say and what they think.

Resources

- Thought and speech bubbles (optional)

What to do

1. The children create a freeze frame (see page 84) of a particular moment in time from a drama, historical project or narrative.

2. The teacher taps one character in the tableau on the shoulder, indicating that the character should speak. The child speaks, in role, saying how he or she feels.

3. The teacher taps other characters of the group in turn.

Variations

● Younger children may like to hold a thought bubble above their heads to indicate they are thinking aloud in character.

● This activity can be developed further by using speech bubbles *and* thought bubbles. The character can first hold up a speech bubble and say something, then hold up a thought bubble and speak his or her thoughts aloud. There may be a mismatch between what a character *says* and what he or she *thinks*! This can be a useful starting point for a discussion.

Additional materials to support this activity can be viewed/downloaded at www.pearsoned.co.uk/glynne

Telephone Conversations

A telephone is a really useful prop for generic drama activities. Telephone conversations can be one- or two-sided. They can be held between children in pairs or between a child and the teacher. This strategy can be used with a whole class or in pairs. Although the activities can be carried out without the props, children – especially in KS1 – do enjoy holding a real telephone!

Suitable for

KS1, KS2

Aims

- To develop listening skills.
- To interrogate a character.

Resources

- Telephone(s) (optional)
- A bell (optional)

What to do

Back to Back

1. In pairs, the children sit back to back and converse. The point is that there are no visual clues and information has to be picked up from tone of voice and by keen listening.

Improvisation

1. Telephones can be used as an integral part of an improvisation. This could be based on scenarios of overheard conversations that might be the impetus for the beginning of an improvisation.

Sitting in a Circle

1. The class sit in a circle.

2. Set out a scenario (see below). Place a telephone on a table in the middle of the circle.

3. Use the bell to mimic the ringing of the phone.

4. Select a child to answer the phone. The class listens to the half of the conversation the child creates.

5. When he or she has finished, ask questions to initiate a discussion. What can be inferred from listening to just one half of a conversation?

Crossed Lines

1. This can be mimed in groups of three.

2. Two people are having a conversation, with a third person listening in.

3. The intruder makes him or herself known.

4. How do the others respond?

Examples of scenarios

Some scenarios for KS1

- A conversation between the three bears.
- Goldilocks calls her mother to tell of her adventure.
- Little Red Riding Hood phones home.
- Jack phones from the top of the beanstalk.
- You call to thank your auntie for a birthday present.

Some scenarios for KS2

- You overhear a telephone conversation that reveals a secret – think how you would react.
- You overhear something unpleasant about yourself – think how you would react.
- You have to make a call to tell your best friend that you cannot make his or her special birthday party.
- You make a call of complaint about a faulty iPod.
- You pick up the phone at home when you told a class member (who you wish to avoid) that you'd be out.

Freeze Frames

These are silent tableaux that show a particular moment in time. They can be used to explore an incident or event in detail. The participants have to consider their facial expressions and body language very carefully and how each of the members of the group relate to one another.

Suitable for

KS1, KS2

Aims

- To introduce a dramatic convention.
- To work cooperatively in a pair or group.
- To recall a key moment in a play, story or point in history in detail.

Resources

- Copy of a play or story (optional)
- Space in which to work, though paired or small group work could take place in a classroom

What to do

1. Tell the children that they are to recreate a scene from a text or an historical period. Each pair or group may select a different point in the text. The sequence of freeze frames could represent a complete narrative or a part of it.

2. The group or pair should consider the emotions they are trying to convey and pay attention to facial expressions and body shape. Then, they get into position and keep still.

3. Sound can be added to the tableau. For example, when the teacher taps a character on the shoulder the child could speak in role, which could be developed into an improvisation.

Variations

- This variation should be demonstrated. The children work in pairs, one sculpting the other into a character. One child is the 'clay' and the other the sculptor. The sculptor gently moulds the clay into position and suggests facial expressions.
- The session – either as set out on page 84 or the sculpting variation – could be started by asking the children to represent a range of emotions that could then be transferred to the tableau, as on page 84. Here are some examples of emotions that you could suggest:
  - anger
  - pride
  - fear
  - joy
  - hate
  - energy
  - laziness
  - happiness
  - despair
  - enthusiasm.

These words could be put onto cards and the children invited to choose an emotion.

Additional materials to support this activity can be viewed/downloaded at **www.pearsoned.co.uk/glynne**

Sculpting

This activity helps to build trust between the children. It should be modelled by the teacher. Initially, it is a paired activity. It is closely related to Freeze Frames (see page 84).

Suitable for

KS1, KS2

Aims

● To develop concentration.
● To develop cooperative ways of working.

Resources

● A large space, such as a hall
● Tambourine (optional)

What to do

1. Introduce the activity by saying that we can sometimes read someone's mood by looking at their body language.
2. Ask the children to spread out in the hall and crouch down. Clap or bang the tambourine and ask them to gradually grow into a 'sad' or 'happy' shape. They should include facial expressions as well as a body outline. So, for example, if they are sad, they may sit with their heads in their hands and an expression of dismay on their faces.
3. The next stage is to ask the children to work in pairs.
4. One child is to 'sculpt' the other into a shape that represents an emotion. You will need to model this and it is important to set ground rules. One

child acts as the sculptor and the other is the 'lump of clay'. The sculptor gently moves the 'clay' into a position that suggests the required emotion (see below for the emotions that they could represent).

5. The children then swap roles so the sculptor becomes the piece of clay.

Emotions that could be represented

- Joy
- Happiness
- Surprise
- Confusion
- Horror
- Anger
- Hatred
- Worry

- Astonishment
- Enjoyment
- Enchantment
- Fascination
- Dread
- Jealousy
- Fear

Variations

- The activity can be carried out as a group sculpture is made. This could be used to represent the theme of a class book. Meaningful cross-curricular links can be made to works of art, such as pieces by Rodin.
- Write the emotions on cards and ask each pair to pick a card to sculpt.
- Each 'statue' changes from a happy to a sad emotion, resulting in a discussion of how different these emotions felt and the differences in body language.

Additional materials to support this activity can be viewed/downloaded at www.pearsoned.co.uk/glynne

Role on the Wall

This is a drama technique that helps children to engage more fully with a text and is particularly useful for character analysis. It enables children to explore layers of meaning which extends their vocabulary and improves their writing.

Suitable for

KS1, KS2

Aims

- To introduce a dramatic convention.
- To develop insight into a character or issue.

Resources

- Large sheets of paper and flipchart pens

What to do

1. Initially, it is probably best to model this technique with the whole class, but, later, you could get the children to work in small groups.

2. Select a character from a story that is being read in class and draw an outline of him or her on a large sheet of paper.

3. The space around the outline can then be filled with comments about the character, such as:

   - how the character feels about himself or herself
   - how the character feels about other people
   - his or her likes and dislikes.

4. If you are working with KS2 children, you may decide to select more than one character from the text. Alternatively, you can fill the space around the outline with comments made by other characters. The space inside the figure can then be used to capture the character's own feelings at particular moments in the text. This can be used to create a focus on the difference between external views of a character and the way that he or she sees himself or herself.

Conscience Alley

This dramatic technique can be used to explore the dilemmas that characters may encounter. By taking on the roles, the children are directly confronted with both sides of an argument. This is a powerful strategy and the children often comment on how it really allows them to enter fully into role. It may be easiest to undertake this activity in a hall rather than a classroom.

Suitable for

KS2

Aims

- To explore a character fully.
- To look at a problem from two points of view.

What to do

1. The children stand in two lines facing one another. Give one child a role to play. The children in one line are to be the voices of one side of the dilemma and the children in the other line are to reflect the opposite point of view.

2. As the child who is in role walks past each child in the lines, he or she makes one brief persuasive point that reflects his or her line's side of the dilemma. The children in the two lines speak alternately. For example, a character may be debating whether to give back some cash that he found by chance.

Side 1: persuading the character to keep the cash	Side 2: persuading the character to return the cash
You know you want to keep it.	You know that money belongs to someone else.
Think of all the things you could buy with a £50 note.	Keeping something that's not yours is theft.
Who will ever know you didn't try to find who it belonged to?	Whoever lost that will really miss that amount of cash.
Only a loser would go to the police.	You know you'll feel guilty if you don't try.

Hats, Glasses and Bags

A box containing a variety of simple props is easy to assemble and invaluable during improvisation sessions. Hats, scarves, glasses and bags are readily available and immediately help to suggest character.

Suitable for

KS1, KS2

Aims

- To develop speaking skills.
- To develop characterisation.

Resources

- Hats – for example, a baby's bonnet, balaclava, baseball cap, chef's hat, trilby, straw hat, flowered hat, swimming cap, beret, policeman's hat, fur hat, woolly hat, top hat.
- Bags – for example, a plastic bag, hessian 'eco' bag, shoulder bag, large shopping bag, satchel, evening bag, briefcase, suitcase, rucksack, a variety of handbags in different styles and colours.
- Glasses – for example, sunglasses, wire-rimmed, old-fashioned National Health Service glasses, gold-rimmed spectacles, small and large frames, plastic and metal frames, pince-nez, half-framed glasses.

What to do

1. Invite the children to pick a prop from the box. The class could be divided into groups. Each member of the group could select a prop. The children then take on the role that the prop suggests. For example, a briefcase might suggest a businessman, wire-rimmed glasses might suggest a character who is susceptible to bullying, a broad-brimmed hat could suggest a wealthy lady or a guest at a wedding.

2. Suggest a scenario where the characters might interact. Here are some ideas:

- meeting in a train carriage
- meeting at a bus stop
- meeting in a lift
- meeting on holiday
- meeting on an aeroplane
- at a shopping centre
- at a party
- at a committee meeting.

3. Ask the children to improvise the scene.

Variations

- The children work in pairs and act out the scenario of meeting accidentally in the street or at an airport.
- Each character gives a short monologue, telling of their life, prompted by the prop selected.
- The objects can be divided into 'angry' or 'happy' props and used to develop specific emotions.
- The children can have props from the same category – that is, everyone having a different bag or wearing a different hat. Each child says one line that encapsulates the character created. A starter line might be, 'My name is ____ and I am angry today because ...' or 'When I wear this hat I feel ...', which, for example, you could model as, 'When I wear this hat I feel special because everyone turns to look at me.' This variation would need to be modelled to ensure that the children know what they need to do.

Marvellous Mimes

These activities help to develop concentration, coordination and cooperation. They can be played at the beginning of a drama session as a warm-up or during spare moments within the classroom. It is useful to have some objects as resources that have no obvious use or old items with which the children will not be familiar. Younger children will need tangible objects but older children can mime without props. Included here are two activities that give different children the chance to lead the rest of the class.

Suitable for

KS1, KS2

Aims

- To develop concentration.
- To develop cooperation in group work.
- To develop imagination.

Resources

- Collection of different artefacts (optional)

What to do

Mimed Objects

1. The class sit in a circle.
2. One child picks up a real or imaginary object – a hairbrush, pen or screwdriver, for example – and, after allowing the rest of the class to identify it from his or her mime, passes the object to the next person who mimes using it in a different way. For example, a screwdriver

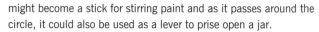

might become a stick for stirring paint and as it passes around the circle, it could also be used as a lever to prise open a jar.

3. Another object is picked up and different uses are mimed as it is passed around the circle.

Guess the Leader

1. A child goes out of the room.

2. The rest of the class form a circle and choose a leader.

3. The child returns to the room.

4. The leader begins to mime a simple action (very slowly) and everyone copies her or his actions.

5. The leader changes the action.

6. The child who went out of the room has to identify who the leader is pretending to be.

Variation

- Follow the Leader, which involves different children taking turns to be the leader. The aim is that the change of leader should take place smoothly, each new child keeping the mime going. An agreed signal may be needed to denote each change of leader.

Chapter 2

Reading

Generic ideas and activities

Book Week

Holding a book week is an exciting way to share and enthuse about books. The whole school can be involved, including parents, teaching assistants, the school office staff and the caretaker, as well as the children and teachers. Events can run for a whole week or be concentrated in one day. These events do need to be planned effectively but are worth the effort as the children are directly engaged in a wide variety of language-based activities.

Suitable for

KS1, KS2

Aim

- To enthuse children about books and reading.

What to do

1. Plan the events which will be held during the week. The book week also needs to be publicised, to parents and possibly the local community.

2. Having a theme for the week can give cohesion to the events. For example, the popularity of the Harry Potter books would lend itself to a magical theme. Other themes are:
    - fairy tales and nursery rhymes
    - monsters
    - mystery and adventure
    - sport
    - animals and pets
    - plays

- poems
- fashion
- music
- dinosaurs
- space
- underwater
- comics and jokes
- characters from TV and film.

3. There should be activities for the whole school. Here are some ideas.

- Competitions – prizes to be awarded in a special assembly. You could have a competition to design a book cover, write a story or poem, create another character to join a favourite story, design a poster and so on.

- A quiz – about a book, film, TV characters and so on and include a 'Who said that?' item.

- Hold a book character assembly – everyone, including the staff, could dress as book characters. For the assembly you could:
  - hold a competition for the most authentic costume – this often proves the highlight of the week
  - invite a storyteller, author or poet to speak to the children
  - ask children to share their work from the week – their stories, poems, plays, examples of storytelling, improvisations
  - ask members of staff to share their favourite books
  - show clips from film versions of books
  - play clips from audio versions of books.

- Buy and swap books by:
  - inviting a bookseller into the school
  - arranging a swap shop – the children swapping books they have read.

4. In the classroom, the following activities work well.

- Storytelling:
  - teachers, parents and other staff tell stories
  - stories in a range of languages can be told by involving multilingual staff and parents.
- Bookmaking:
  - make books with the children that tie in with the theme
  - the books can be shared in the assembly
  - displays of the books can be set up in classrooms and in communal areas of the school.
- Films:
  - watch the film versions of books, comparing and contrasting them
  - make short films using simple video cameras
  - show the films in assembly.
- Poems:
  - create collections of poems
  - ask the children to pick their favourites and read them aloud
  - write class poems on the book week's theme.

5. Invite guests to the school. If the budget permits, the children find such events memorable if an author or other outside guest comes, such as a poet, storyteller, theatre group, puppeteer, librarian, journalist, illustrator, someone who works in film or TV.

6. Some other activities worth considering include:

- hiring a badge-making machine – the children can make badges of their favourite characters
- visiting the local library
- visiting the local bookshop.

Early Word Games

These activities help early readers to recognise a range of words on sight. They offer a lively way to engage in interactive reading activities, either in pairs or groups.

Suitable for

KS1

Aim

- To develop sight vocabulary.

Resources

- A set of picture cards and word cards, plus a duplicated set
- Board games, such as Ludo or Snakes and Ladders

What to do

Matching Pairs

1. The aim of this classic game is to find matching pairs. Initially, the game could be introduced by using picture cards of familiar objects. The word cards could be introduced gradually. This game is useful for reinforcing vocabulary that has been introduced in other curriculum areas.

2. To play, a set of cards is placed face down on a table.

3. The first child turns over two cards, says what is on each and sees if they match. If they do not, the child puts them back in the same place, face down.

4. When a child finds a matching pair, he or she keeps the cards.

5. The child with the greatest number of matching sets wins the game.

Moving Along

1. To play this game, set out a popular board game such as Ludo or Snakes and Ladders.

2. Play the chosen game in the usual way, but, instead of rolling a dice and moving the counter, the child picks up a word card. If it is read correctly, the child can move his or her counter, moving one space for each letter of the word. For example, 'house' has five letters, so the player would move along five spaces on the board.

3. The cards can be made using several different colours. As an alternative to counting the number of letters in a word, each colour could denote a different number of moves. So, a red card could be five moves, a blue card four moves and so on.

Rub Me Out

1. This game can be played in groups. It is important to differentiate the lists for different groups.

2. Write a list of familiar words on an interactive whiteboard or flipchart.

3. A child comes up to the list and says a word that he or she can read, then erases the word from the board.

4. The next child comes up and repeats the process.

5. To add an extra fun element, the class can be timed to see how quickly the children can get through the list.

Walking About

We are surrounded by the printed word. Early readers need to develop an awareness of print and understand that it conveys meaning. Taking the class on a word walk is a practical and engaging way to do this.

Suitable for

KS1

Aims

- To begin to recognise printed words in a variety of settings.
- To develop an understanding that print conveys meaning.

What to do

Initial sessions: out and about

1. Take the class on a word walk. This could be around the school or into the local area.

2. Point out print in the environment. Talk about the signs and symbols that can be seen and why they are there – road signs, shop signs, notices and so on.

3. Emphasise prepositional language – *across* the road, *by* the sweet shop, *past* the library, *under* the bridge, *next to* the supermarket and so on.

4. Back in the classroom, make cards with signs, symbols and labels for the children to play matching games.

5. Ask the children to make signs and labels for the classroom that are similar to those they saw on their walk, such as no entry signs, a warning sign, a first aid sign, instructions for use and so on.

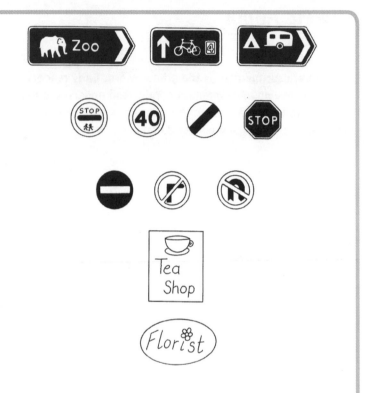

Follow up: role-play area

1. Set up a new role-play area – a garage, for example.
2. Discuss what might be in the garage.
3. If possible, visit a garage. What signs and print can the children see?
4. In shared sessions, make some signs together.
5. The children can write lists of work to be carried out, bills, design posters to advertise the garage, write cheques and pay the bills.

Variation

- Other ideas for a role-play area include a supermarket, shoe shop, clothes shop, doctors' surgery, café, hairdresser, newsagent, travel agent, airport, railway station, post office, office, chemist, dry cleaner, hotel reception.

Guided Reading Activities

These ideas help children to extend their understanding of the texts they are reading. They are designed to be used in a very flexible way. You could introduce one of the activities after a guided reading session or one or more could be included as part of the session. They are particularly useful if you organise your sessions as reading workshops and need the other groups to be involved in purposeful and meaningful activities.

Suitable for

KS1

Aims

- To reflect on books that have been read.
- To develop comprehension skills.

Resources

- Paper, felt-tip pens, pencils
- Activity cards (optional)
- Reading journals (optional)

What to do

1. Try asking the children to do some of the following activities.
   - *What Could Happen Next?* Draw a picture for a new last page.
   - *Make a Model* Make a model of one of the scenes in the book, using Playmobil, Lego and so on.
   - *Think of a Question* Ask or write a question about something in the book. Can your friend find the answer? Now swap over – can you answer your friend's question?

- *Pick a Page* Choose a page in your book and read it to a friend. Can he or she guess what comes next? Now swap.

- *Factfinding* Find two facts in your book. Tell them to your friend.

- *Who Am I?* Play this with a friend, using the characters from the book. Can they follow your clues and guess which character you are? Take turns to play.

- *Describe and Draw* Describe a character to a friend. Can your friend then draw a picture of that character in his or her reading journal? Now swap over.

- *Story Map* Draw a story map for your story in your reading journal.

- *Role Play* Retell the story with the rest of your group as the characters.

- *Hot Seating* One person in your group can pretend to be one of the characters and you can ask him or her questions.

- *What Does it Mean?* Find three words in your book that you are not sure about. Use a dictionary to help you work out what they mean. Write down the words and their meanings.

Variation

- Some of these ideas could be adapted to use with independent reading. They could be linked to the home–school programme to help parents be aware of the range of activities that can be developed from a book.

See **www.pearsoned.co.uk/glynne** for material on guided reading prompts.

Blooming Questions

In order for them to be effective readers, we need children to be able to read for meaning. To do this, they need many opportunities to respond to a range of questions that will help to develop their comprehension skills.

Suitable for

KS1, KS2

Aims

- To develop comprehension skills.
- To evaluate a text critically.
- To develop questioning skills.

Resources

- Posters with sample questions or question starters
- Question cards, prompt cards or a question cube (optional)

What to do

1. Initially with younger children, you will probably want to focus on literal questions – ones that deal with recalling facts. If their abilities to understand texts are to develop, however, you will want to move on to more complex questions. One way to do this is to link the questions to Bloom's Taxonomy (first presented in 1956).

2. Bloom identified six levels of thinking, from simply recalling facts, as the lowest level, to more complex and abstract levels, the highest of these being evaluation. Each level or layer builds on the previous one. So, for example:

- before you can *understand* a concept or fact you must be able to *remember* it
- before you can *apply* a concept you need to be able to *understand* it.

3. We have a tendency to ask questions at the knowledge level, but it is important that we use the higher levels, too. The questions linked to Bloom's Taxonomy (see examples on page 113) show how children need to think more deeply and provide more extensive answers as they progress from the initial knowledge questions to the evaluation ones.

4. It is a good idea to have posters displayed in the classroom with examples of question starters. These can be used to introduce the different types of questions and then the children can refer to them on a regular basis. You may decide to use only a few of the levels with younger children, but, with older children, you can discuss how the higher-level questions can help them to gain a deeper understanding of a text.

5. It is important that this approach is used in a relaxed atmosphere as you do not want the children to feel that they are being interrogated, so try not to barrage them with lots of questions. The idea is to ask just a few questions in order to stimulate a discussion. For more reticent children, you may want to begin with the Talking about Books activity on page 144.

Variations

- Put some of the question starters on cards to use as prompts during guided reading. The children could then pick a card and either answer a question or create their own question.
- Use large blank dice or cardboard cubes. Write a different prompt on each face of the cube. For example, 'Who?', 'What?', 'Where?', 'Which?', 'Why?', 'How?'. Give each child a turn to roll the dice or cube and to think of a question to ask his or her partner or the rest of the group.

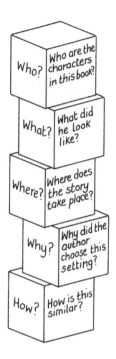

Who? Who are the characters in this book?

What? What did he look like?

Where? Where does the story take place?

Why? Why did the author choose this setting?

How? How is this similar?

Examples of questions linked to Bloom's Taxonomy

- Knowledge
  - Where does the story take place?
  - What does he look like?
  - Who are the characters in the book?
- Simple comprehension
  - What do you think is happening here?
  - Which part of the story do you like best?
  - What might this word or phrase mean?
- Application
  - Which stories have openings like this?
  - Can you think of another story that has a similar theme, such as good over evil?

- Analysis
  - What makes you think that?

  - Can you explain why …?

  - Why did the author choose this setting?
- Synthesis
  - What is your opinion? What evidence do you have to support your view?

  - Given what you know about … what do you think?
- Evaluation
  - What makes this a successful story?

  - How is it similar to …?

  - Which is better and why?

Additional materials to support this activity can be viewed/downloaded at **www.pearsoned.co.uk/glynne**

Prompts for Fiction

The teacher's role in guided reading is vitally important. You can support the development of the children's comprehension skills by guiding and prompting them during discussions. Written comprehension exercises do not move them forward in any way – they just confirm their levels of understanding.

Suitable for

KS2, some fluent readers in KS1

Aims

- To develop comprehension skills.
- To develop a personal response.
- To develop the ability to reflect on a text critically.

Resources

- Texts
- Question prompt cards (see **www.pearsoned.co.uk/glynne**)

What to do

1. Introduce the prompt cards after the children have read the text. For some more reticent children you may need to model a response, for example, '*I thought that the most important character was ... because ...*'. In pairs, ask the children to discuss their opinions and then share them with the rest of the group. (See page 116 for some examples of prompts for different aspects of fiction texts.)

2. Next give each pair a different prompt card. They can talk about their ideas before explaining them to the other children. Alternatively, put the cards in a pile and the children can take turns picking up one of them. It is important to ask them to justify their opinions and ideas by

referring back to the text, for example, 'Where is the evidence for that?' This aspect will probably have to be modelled on several occasions as children can find this quite difficult at first.

3. Over time, you can ask the pairs to create their own prompts or questions.

Examples of prompts for fiction

Setting

- Where does the story take place?
- Is the setting really important to the story or could it have happened anywhere?
- Do any words or phrases help you to imagine the place where the story was set?

Character

- Who is the most important character in the story?
- What sort of character is he or she?
- Would you like to get to know this character?
- Is there anything you would like to ask a character in this story?

Plot

- What are the problems in this story?
- How do they get sorted out?
- How would you have sorted them out?
- Which is the key event in the story?

Theme

- What do you think this book is about?
- Why do you think the author wrote this book?
- Have you read any other stories that have a similar theme?

Author

- Do you know of any other books by this author?
- Does this author always write like this?

Additional materials to support this activity can be viewed/downloaded at
www.pearsoned.co.uk/glynne

In addition, prompts for **poetry**, **plays** and **non-fiction** are available on the above
website.

Reading Journals

> A reading journal provides an opportunity for children to reflect on their reading. Making entries in the journal should not be regarded as a chore but as a useful tool. Guided reading provides a good opportunity to give the children a chance to talk about their reading when they can use their journal notes to articulate their thoughts about the text.

Suitable for

KS1, KS2

Aims

- To reflect on books that have been read.
- To develop a personal response.

Resources

- Notebooks – special ones if possible, rather than exercise books

What to do

1. Introduce the concept of reading journals to the class or group.
2. Discuss what could be included in the journal and demonstrate how it might look.
3. The following may be included for the different key stages.

   #### For Key Stage 1

   - The journal may be a class or group book to which the children contribute. It might be in the form of a big book or even an audio recording or a document on the computer that is added to regularly.

- Fiction activities
  - Drawings of characters from stories with key associated words.
  - Drawings of settings from stories.
  - Story maps.
  - Storyboards showing the beginning, middle and end.
  - Answers to the following questions: How did you feel about the characters in the story? Which characters did you like? Why? Were you happy with the ending of the story?
- Non-fiction activities
  - New facts learned.
  - Notes on the most useful part of a book – its diagrams, pictures, glossary, index, for example.
  - Most interesting information learned from a book.

For Key Stage 2

- The following format could be used to record information.

Overview

Date	Book read (title, author)	How I wish to develop my reading	What I have learned

Content

- The beginning of the book
  - What do you think of the characters so far?
  - What do you think the story will be about?
  - Note down anything that you don't understand.
- Midway through the book
  - Have you changed your mind about any of the characters?
  - Is the story developing as you thought it might?
  - Have you found it easy to read? Is it enjoyable? If not, why not?

- Ending
  - Was the end of the book satisfactory or did you find it disappointing? Why was that?
  - Did the book end as you had predicted?
- Recommendation
  - Would you recommend this book to a friend? If so, what did you like? Were the characters believable? Was the story a 'page turner'?
  - On a scale of 1 to 10 (10 is the highest mark), how would you rate this book?

4. The following are some ideas that could be included in the journal.

- Fiction:
  - story maps
  - cartoon strips
  - lists of words used to create atmosphere, suspense, excitement
  - story graphs
  - emotions graphs
  - story skeletons
  - drawings of characters
  - storyboards
  - extracts from stories.
- Non-fiction:
  - diagrams
  - mind maps
  - newly learned facts
  - notes on where to locate useful information.

Activities for Reading Journals (KS1)

Through these activities you can assess children's understanding and enjoyment of the books that they are reading. See page 118 for general information about reading journals.

(See www.pearsoned.co.uk/glynne for complimentary activities for KS2.)

Suitable for

KS1

Aims

- To reflect on books that have been read.
- To develop a personal response.

Resources

- Reading journals

What to do

1. The journal could be a whole-class book, but you take responsibility for the writing process to enable the children to concentrate on their ideas and responses. Alternatively, each guided group could have its own collaborative journal. This is useful when children are being introduced to journals.

2. It is important to vary the types of tasks that are given to the children – they do not need to take the form of written tasks (see page 122 for some ideas).

Some ideas for reading journal activities

For fiction

- Draw a picture of your favourite part of the story. Write a sentence to say why you liked it.
- Draw a picture of something important that happened in your story. Can you label it?
- Draw a picture of your favourite character in the story.
- Make a list of the main characters in your book. Can you write a describing word for each one?
- Draw a story map of your favourite book. Ask someone to guess what it is.
- Describe the setting of your story in your own words.
- Choose one of the main characters and say how he or she is feeling. Can you give a reason for your answer?
- Can you write a different ending for your story?

For non-fiction

- Write down two new facts that you have found.
- Draw a picture or diagram of the most interesting thing you have learned.
- Write a glossary for some of the new words in your book.
- Look in your book and write a question for your partner. Can he or she find the answer?

DARTs

Standing for **Directed Activities Related to Text**, these interactive activities help to develop comprehension skills and critical readers as an awareness of how a text is put together is gained. DARTs activities are ideal for guided reading sessions and collaborative work. The approach can be applied to subjects across the curriculum.

Suitable for

KS2

Aims

- To develop comprehension.
- To evaluate a text critically.

Resources

- A range of different texts, including poems, magazine articles, newspaper articles, pamphlets, extracts from novels, extracts from textbooks for history, geography and so on
- Coloured or highlighter pens or pencils

What to do

1. Begin by using a poem as the key text.
2. Read the poem together as a group.
3. Use one or more of the following DARTs strategies in a range of sessions or as follow-up work. Not all the activities can be applied to all texts – some adapt more easily to non-fiction. Some work well electronically. An example of several of the techniques being applied to a poem is given in the box on page 124–5.

Underlining or highlighting

1. Use one or more colours to highlight words or phrases relating to a particular theme. Either coloured pens or the highlight tool on a computer could be used.

Segmenting

1. Divide the poem or text into sections then look at each in turn and see how they relate to each other.

Labelling

1. Give each verse or section a title.
2. Give each verse or section an alternative title in the form of a question.

Grouping or ranking

1. Ask which is the most worrying or annoying or descriptive verse or section.

Listing

1. List words that fit the theme.
2. Make a list of words or phrases that raise questions.

Tables

1. Some texts lend themselves to being analysed by categorising the elements in the form of a table.

Example of DARTs activities being used to analyse a poem

Summer is Gone

I have but one story –
The stags are moaning,
The sky is snowing,
Summer is gone.

Quickly the low sun
Goes drifting down
Behind the rollers,
Lifting and long.

The wild geese cry
Down the storm
The ferns have fallen
Russet and torn.

The wings of the birds
Are clotted with ice.
I have but one story –
Summer is gone.

Anon, in Michael Rosen, *A World of Poetry* (Kingfisher, 1991)

Underlining or highlighting

- Highlight all the *verbs*. How do they help to evoke the mood of the poem?
- Highlight the names of *animals* in another colour. In what way does the variety of animals mentioned help to build a picture of the countryside?
- Highlight the *adjectives* in a third colour. How do they help to build the picture and convey the mood?

Labelling

- Give each verse or section a title.

Grouping or ranking

- Rank the verses in order of level of dismay (that summer is over).

Additional activities can be found at **www.pearsoned.co.uk/glynne**

Get the Idea

It is important for children to be able to identify the main idea and supporting details when they are reading texts, particularly non-fiction ones, and this activity enables them to do this.

Suitable for

KS2

Aims

- To locate and retrieve relevant information from fiction and non-fiction texts.
- To refer to the text to support an idea.

Resources

- Extracts from information or fiction texts
- Pencils, highlighters or felt-tip pens
- Interactive whiteboard (optional)

What to do

1. You may want to model this task initially so that the children understand the concepts of a main idea and supporting details (see worked example on page 127). Enlarge a text (or display it on an interactive whiteboard) and explain to the children that the main idea is the most important idea in a paragraph. Then the details in the other sentences help to describe or explain the main idea.

2. Read the first paragraph through with the children and then model how to locate the main idea and supporting details. To make this clear, you could highlight the main idea in one colour and the details in another.

3. Ask the children to talk with their partners to decide where the main idea is in the next paragraph. Can they locate the supporting details? The children can then share their thoughts with the rest of the class.

4. Next, give the pairs of children a similar text and ask them to read through the whole text first before trying to locate the main idea and details in each paragraph. They could highlight the sentences or underline them with felt-tip pens. The children could then note down the information that they have located on a writing frame or graphic organiser (see box on page 128).

5. The task can be differentiated by giving some pairs of children other texts – either simpler or more complex. Alternatively, some children could concentrate on just one paragraph while other pairs analyse two or more paragraphs.

Worked example

Niagara Falls

Niagara Falls is one of the most beautiful sights in North America. It is on the Niagara River about halfway between Lake Ontario and Lake Erie. Niagara Falls is on the American and Canadian border. The American Falls is 51 metres high. On the Canadian side, the Horseshoe Falls is 49 metres high.

Main idea

- Niagara Falls is one of the most beautiful sights in North America.

Supporting details

- The American Falls is 51 metres high.
- Niagara Falls is on the American and Canadian border.

Source: http://studyzone.org/testprep/ela4/h/supportingdetailsl.cfm

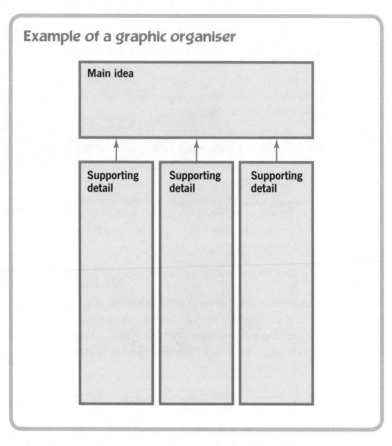

Example of a graphic organiser

To download the above resource, see **www.pearsoned.co.uk/glynne**

Phonics

Draw a Rhyme

This activity reinforces early phonic knowledge linked to CVC words.

Suitable for

KS1

Aim

- To develop phonological awareness.

Resources

- Set of CVC word cards, for example, *lad, mug, hop, dad, ten, pet, run, sad, tell, shop, shed, met, hug, fat, shell, bug, hat, bun, men, bin, sun, fell, bat, thin, rug, cat, bed, wet, pop, dig, hen, bell, ted, big, tin, pen, fun, vet, fin, pig, top, mad, wig, red* (see example at **www.pearsoned.co.uk/glynne**)
- Mini-whiteboards and pens

What to do

1. Place the cards face up so the children can see the words. The children could work in pairs to find two cards that rhyme, for example, *'sad'* and *'dad'* or *'fun'* and *'bun'*. Next, they need to produce a drawing for the two words together.

Sad dad

Fun bun

2. You could get the children to think of additional rhyming words either to extend the existing set or to make a new set, for example, CCVC words (*crab/grab, clock/block, spin/twin*).

Variation

• Simplify the game by just asking the children to pick up any two words, read them and then draw a picture to illustrate them.

Peel the Post-it!

This lively activity gives the opportunity to reinforce the teaching of phonemes and provides a chance to assess understanding. It can involve the whole class or a small group. The children really enjoy the anticipation of revealing the next sound by peeling the Post-it!

Suitable for

KS1

Aims

- To apply the teaching of phonemes.
- Assessment for learning – this activity will allow you to assess whether the children have understood the phonics teaching and are able to apply it.

Resources

- A packet of sticky Post-it notes
- An artefact that can be passed around, such as a stone, a ball etc.

What to do

1. Prepare the pack of sticky Post-it notes in advance. Write a range of phonemes on each note. You could prepare several packs at different levels.
2. The children sit in a circle – the sticky note pack is placed in the centre face down.
3. Pass the artefact around the circle.
4. When you give a signal – by banging a tambourine or saying 'Stop' – the child who has the artefact moves to the centre of the circle and has to show the sticky note, sound the phoneme and give a word beginning with the sound.

5. That sticky note is peeled from the pack and put to one side. The artefact is passed around again until each child has a turn at peeling a Post-it.

The Name Game

This activity reinforces the teaching of phonemes and adds a broader dimension to phonics teaching.

Suitable for

Upper KS1, KS2

Aim

- To reinforce phonics teaching.

Resources

- A list of categories – for example:

Food	Fruit	Boy's name	Girl's name	Transport	Country

What to do

1. Working in teams, pairs or individually, the children have to find a word (noun) containing the appropriate phoneme. They can use the Internet or books to assist.

   Example: the phoneme is 'long vowel a-e, ai, ay'.

Food	Fruit	Boy's name	Girl's name	Transport	Country
plaice	grape	James	Jane	train	Spain

   Give points for each correct word. This works particularly well as a team game and promotes good discussion when equally suitable alternatives are found – for example 'plane' is an acceptable mode of transport (instead of 'train').

Variation

- A time element can be added – this works well when playing in teams.

Tops and Tails

This interactive game helps to develop vocabulary and phonemic awareness.

Suitable for

Upper KS1, KS2

Aims

- To enhance vocabulary.
- To consolidate phonemic awareness.
- To develop listening skills.

What to do

1. The children sit in a circle.
2. The first child says a given word.
3. The next child has to continue with a word that begins with the final sound of the previous word.

   For example:

   Given word – 'plu**m**',
   Next child – 'mil**k**',
   Next child – 'kin**g**'

Variation

- The game is more challenging if the words belong to a specific category, for example, linking to a current class project or perhaps words associated with sport, fashion, food, animals, etc.

Countdown

This is a version of the popular TV game. Children enjoy the excitement of working against the clock to create words. This activity can be played as a group game, with the whole class, or individually.

Suitable for

Upper KS1, KS2

Aims

- To apply learned phonics skills.
- To aid spelling.
- To gain an appreciation of how words are constructed.

Resources

- A selection of letter cards – vowels and consonants
- Removable adhesive such as masking tape or sticky tack
- A timer (a traditional egg timer works particularly well as it is very visual)
- Mini-whiteboards

What to do

1. One child selects eight letter cards – a combination of vowels and consonants – and places them on a board with removable adhesive for all to see.

2. The timer is started to countdown for one minute.

3. On their mini-whiteboards in pairs, groups or individually, the children make a word using as many of the selected letters as possible.

4. Award points for the longest word.

Variations

- Use magnetic boards, individually or in pairs.
- Introduce an extra element of challenge – beat the teacher!

Fiction and poetry activities

Talking about Books

It is important for children to be able to read between and beyond the lines. They need to understand authors' implied meanings and evaluate the authors' craft. To help children do this, we need to provide plenty of opportunities to discuss books. The 'Book-talk' approach was developed by Aidan Chambers (*Tell Me: Children, Reading and Talk*, Thimble Press, 2001) to provide an opportunity for children to explore their personal and collective responses to a text. Book-talk helps them to develop the confidence to offer ideas and extend thinking. They are also encouraged to raise questions as well as make points and suggestions.

Suitable for

KS1, KS2

Aims

- To develop comprehension skills.
- To develop the skills of inference and deduction.
- To reflect on books that have been read.

Resources

- Prompt cards (optional)

What to do

1. Developing comprehension skills can sometimes be a difficult balancing act. We want to provide opportunities for children to discuss texts, but we do not want them to feel that they are being bombarded with questions.

2. Like many strategies, in order for it to be successful, Book-talk needs to be modelled. You need to *think aloud* and demonstrate how to talk effectively about a book. Then, when eliciting responses from the children, it helps to use a phrase such as, 'Tell me about …'. Here are some other useful prompts.

- Was there anything you liked about this book?
- Was there anything you disliked?
- Was there anything that puzzled you?
- Were there any puzzles – any connections – that you noticed?
- Have you read any other books like this? How did they compare?
- Which parts of the book stay in your mind most clearly?
- How did the main character change?
- What surprises are there in the book?

3. By using these open-ended prompts, the children are encouraged to express their *feelings* regarding the text. This enables them to engage with texts and begin to explore their meaning.

What Can You See?

Interacting with picture books teaches children valuable skills, as well as being an enjoyable experience.

Introduction

Different skills are required when reading a picture book from those used for a written text. All picture books use illustration as well as words to convey meaning and, by encountering different styles of illustration, children are able to develop their visual literacy skills. These are important as so much information is given through visual imagery, on television and on the Internet.

The best picture books are multilayered. They demonstrate that authors and illustrators interact with the reader not just through words but also through images. For example, in the work of John Burningham and Anthony Browne, there are often two stories or viewpoints running side by side – one in the text and another in the illustrations.

Some people mistakenly think that picture books are just for young children, but there are now many examples of very sophisticated books aimed at older readers (see the Further sources of information section at the end of this activity). By encouraging children to interact with picture books, you can show how a 'text' can be revisited so that the deeper layers of meaning can be accessed. Having discussions with the children can develop a closer understanding of setting, mood, characterisation and narrative structure. It is also easy to locate the evidence in the text to support and develop their thinking.

Suitable for

KS1, KS2

Aims

- To enthuse children about books and reading.
- To help them develop comprehension skills.
- To enable them to become critical readers.

Resources

- A variety of good-quality picture books

What to do

1. The Book-talk approach is an ideal one to use with picture books (see page 144). Here are some examples of generic prompts that you can use.
   - Do the words and pictures tell the same story?
   - What do the pictures do that the words cannot?
   - Which part of the picture do you notice most?
   - Have you a favourite/least favourite picture?
2. Ask the children to study a picture book in pairs. As they go through the book slowly and carefully, one child concentrates on the illustrations while the other concentrates on the text. When they have finished, they close the book and orally reconstruct the story together.

Further sources of information

- There are some excellent suggestions for discussing picture books in the Booktrust resource pack 'Looking at Books – the Big Picture Guide to Exploring Picture Books' (see **http://fileserver.booktrust.org.uk/usr/resources/239/looking-at-books-the-big-picture-guide-to-exploring-picture-books.pdf**)
- The Booktrust Resource Pack for Book Week also has some useful guidance (see **www.booktrust.org.uk/books-and-reading/children/childrens-book-week**)
- Two other useful publications are:
  - Judith Graham, *Cracking Good Picture Books*, NATE, 2004 (for KS1)
  - Elaine Moss, *Picture Books 9–13: A Signal Bookguide*, 3rd edition, Thimble Press, 1992 (KS2).

Six Hats for Reading

This idea is based on Edward de Bono's Six Thinking Hats (see page 61), which are used to generate different ways of thinking.

Suitable for

KS1, KS2

Aims

- To develop comprehension skills.
- To reflect on books that have been read.
- To evaluate a text critically.

Resources

- Coloured cards (red, yellow, black, green, white and blue) or the children can wear coloured hats or PE bands

What to do

1. Each hat represents a different type of thinking (see pages 62–3 for more information). The six hats can be used to explore a particular aspect of a book.
2. The group discusses an idea, with everyone focusing on one type of thinking at a time, for example:
   - *Red hat* feelings. What are our feelings about this?
   - *Yellow hat* strengths. What are the good points?
   - *Black hat* weaknesses. What is wrong with this?
   - *Green hat* new ideas. What is possible?
   - *White hat* information. What are the facts?
   - *Blue hat* thinking. What thinking is needed?

3. Once the children are familiar with this activity, they can begin to devise their own questions for each colour, such as the following.

- *Red hat* How did you feel about the main character?
- *Yellow hat* What did the author do to make the story interesting?
- *Black hat* How could the book have been improved?
- *Green hat* How could you change the story?
- *White hat* What facts are you given?
- *Blue hat* Can you summarise your thoughts about the story?

Getting to Know You

Giving young children opportunities to talk about the stories that have been read to them and they are beginning to read for themselves is important. This collection of activities allows the children to revisit stories and begin to develop an understanding of character.

Suitable for

KS1

Aims

- To identify and discuss characters from stories.
- To begin to speculate about characters' behaviour.

Resources

- A collection of story books

What to do

1. Choose one or more from the following selection of activities.

   - Model the following game for the children. Think of a character and the children in the class have to ask questions in order to guess who you are thinking of. Examples of useful questions are the following.

     - Are you thinking of a man, woman, girl, boy or animal?

     - Where does the character live?

     - Is the character good or bad?

   - Pin the name of a character on to the back of a child. The child asks the class questions in order to guess who the character is.

- Make some simple drawings of characters from stories known to the children. Write key phrases that the characters have said in the stories onto speech bubbles. The children can then match the speech bubbles to the correct story characters.

- Draw a simple table, as in the example on page 152. Put characteristics and associated vocabulary and phrases onto cards. Ask the children to match the characteristics to the appropriate character in the table. Some children can do this verbally.

Cinderella	Ugly Sisters	Fairy Godmother
hardworking	bossy	kind
sad	unkind	magical
rags	noisy	carriage
fireside	lazy	pumpkin

- Draw an outline of a character and ask the children to write key words and phrases around the outside, following discussion.

- Draw pictures of characters from stories. Ask the children to write a short caption under each, including their names, what they do and what happens to them in the story.

- Ask the children what advice they would give to a character. For example, 'Should Cinderella do all the work?' and 'What would you have said to the Gingerbread Man about the fox?'

What Happens Next?

Prediction is a key reading skill. It necessitates reflecting on what has happened and considering what the likely outcome might be. This activity can be part of a guided reading session or used as a whole-class lesson.

Suitable for

KS1

Aim

- To give children practice in developing prediction skills.

Resources

- Story books, including traditional tales (see below)

Examples of stories that could be used for this activity

First stories	Animal tales	Magical tales
Goldilocks and the Three Bears	The Three Billy Goats Gruff	The Magic Porridge Pot
The Three Little Pigs	The Town Mouse and the Country Mouse	The Princess and the Pea
The Gingerbread Man		Jack and the Beanstalk
The Little Red Hen	The Tortoise and the Hare	The Frog Prince
Little Red Riding Hood		The Elves and the Shoemaker
The Enormous Turnip		Rumplestiltskin

What to do

1. Read part of a story, then ask the children to imagine that they are the main character. What would they do next? Here are some examples of the questions you could ask for particular stories.

   - The Little Red Hen
     If you needed some help in the garden and your friends were too lazy to assist, would you carry on alone or give up?

   - Jack and the Beanstalk
     If you woke up and saw an enormous beanstalk outside your window would you tell your parents, hide under the bedclothes or go outside and climb the beanstalk?

   - The Elves and the Shoemaker
     If you came downstairs and found all your work had been completed, would you stay up each night and watch to see what happened or just enjoy the fact that something magical had occurred?

2. Discuss the children's contributions, then encourage them to refer back to the text to remind themselves what actually happened.

3. Alternatively, play 'What might have happened next?' at a key point in the story. The children then list or draw the possible outcomes.

4. Read on and compare the actual outcome with the 'possibilities' list.

Variation

- When a range of stories have been read, ask the children to discuss any common themes they have noticed. This could be in relation to character, plot or language. For example, did they notice 'the rule of three' for the Three Bears, the Three Billy Goats Gruff and the Three Little Pigs? This literary device can later be replicated in their own writing.

What Is She Like?

This technique encourages children to interact with texts. It helps them to develop an understanding of character and enrich their story writing.

Suitable for

KS1

Aims

- To develop comprehension skills.
- To identify and discuss characters from stories.
- To begin to think about characters' behaviour, appearance, likes and dislikes.

Resources

- Writing frame or sentence starters (see page 156 for examples)

What to do

1. This is a post-reading activity, to do after shared or guided reading. It can be used with any text, but it is important that the children know the story well.

2. In pairs or small groups, the children take on the roles of the characters. It is best to give the children a suggested scene from the story so that they can think about what their characters might say or do. For example, for Jack and the Beanstalk, the children could take on the roles of Jack and his mother, then think about the part of the story when Jack comes back home with the beans. What would his mother say? How would she feel? What would Jack do?

3. The children then use a writing frame or some sentence starters to help them write some information about their characters. For example, *I am*

> Jack's mother, *I live* in a small cottage next to a field and *I have* very
> old clothes because I have no money.
>
> **4.** It helps to model how to use the writing frame or sentence starters,
> particularly as the children may have to imagine some of the facts.
> The role play should help with this aspect.
>
> **5.** Also model how the sentence starters can be changed or edited –
> they are there to help the children, not restrict them. You may need
> to demonstrate how the sentences can be expanded to include more
> information.
>
> **6.** The children can also work with a partner to see if they can think of
> any other sentence starters.
>
> **7.** The writing frame or sentence starters can also be used to support
> story writing, for example, to help them when they are inventing their
> own characters.

Examples of sentence starters

I am . . . .

I live . . . .

I have . . . .

I like . . . .

I don't like . . . .

I wish . . . .

How Do They Feel?

The range of emotions that a character experiences throughout a story can be represented graphically in a similar way to the plot profile described on page 166. This is particularly useful when the central character in a novel undergoes a number of trials. Harry's experiences in the Harry Potter novels and those of Lyra in the *His Dark Materials* trilogy exemplify this well.

Suitable for

KS2

Aims

- To analyse a character's feelings.
- To develop an understanding of how a character is created.

Resources

- Character word tables (see page 158)
- Emotions circle pro forma (see page 159)
- Pens and pencils

What to do

1. Discuss the range of emotions that a character experiences in the story. Use the word tables (see page 158 to aid this process).

2. Discuss how the character's behaviour changes in relation to how he or she feels.

3. Ask the children to complete an emotions circle (see page 159).

4. Alternatively, they could create a feelings chart.

Character word tables

Positive emotions and characteristics

General	Happy, dazzling, jovial, ecstatic, exhilarated, full of beans, glad, jolly, over the moon, animated, merry, pleased, sparkling, sunny, thrilled, vivacious, responsive
Enthusiastic and **interested** characteristics	Keen, eager, willing, excited, foolhardy, impulsive, animated, fanatical, passionate, prepared to have a go, reckless, earnest, fascinated, intrigued, captivated, absorbed
Confident characteristics	Bold, brave, fearless, courageous, determined, daring, heroic, undaunted, self-reliant, intrepid, fearless, valiant, headstrong, enterprising, plucky

Negative emotions and characteristics

General	Sad, disconsolate, unhappy, flat, gloomy, downhearted, glum, melancholy, miserable, sombre, sullen, wretched, depressed, dejected, discouraged
Characteristics associated with **fear**	Worried, anxious, afraid, alarmed, cautious, frightened, nervous, panicky, petrified, terrified, suspicious, timid, doubtful, diffident, cowardly
Characteristics associated with **anger**	Defiant, annoyed, cross, furious, infuriated, livid, mad, enraged, offended, resentful, wild, up in arms, irate, beside yourself, fuming, incensed

Emotions circle

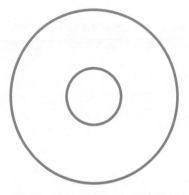

- Write the name of the character from the book you have been reading recently in the centre of the circle.
- How many words can you think of to describe how the character felt in the story? Write them down in the outer circle.
- Do the character's emotions change at different points of the story? Why do you think this might be?
- How do the character's feelings affect the way he or she reacts to other characters?

Variation

- Write each emotion on a separate card. Place the cards face down on a table. Ask each child in turn to take a card and evaluate the character's behaviour in relation to the prompt.

Additional materials to support this activity can be viewed/downloaded at **www.pearsoned.co.uk/glynne**

Wanted!

This activity helps children to analyse a character's behaviour and how it can affect other characters.

Suitable for

KS1, can be adapted for KS2

Aims

- To identify and discuss characters from stories.
- To begin to think about characters' behaviour and actions.
- To analyse a character's feelings.

Resources

- Whiteboard or flipchart or interactive whiteboard
- A3 paper and felt-tip pens

What to do

1. This is a post-reading activity that can be used with any well-known story or book (for how to adapt it for Key Stage 2 children, see Variations at the end of this activity). Choose one of the characters from the story – it is generally best to choose one of the main characters but when the children become experienced in the activity, you can choose a more minor character.

2. Discuss the character's actions in the story. How did he or she behave? Why did he or she ... (*eat Grandma/go into the Three Bears' cottage/ attack the Big Billy Goat Gruff*)? The children could discuss their ideas with a partner before sharing them with the class.

3. Explain to the children that they are going to produce a 'Wanted!' poster (see page 161 for an example). Model this next stage, but also ask the children for suggestions so that they are active participants.

4. The children can then work with a partner to produce their own poster. They can either all produce a poster for the same character or some could think about a different character in the story.

Example of a 'Wanted!' poster

Variations

- Older children can choose a character from a nursery rhyme and discuss his or her actions, asking, for example, *'Why did Humpty Dumpty sit on the wall?'* He could be wanted for wasting the soldiers' time. Here are some other suggestions:
  - spider – for frightening Miss Muffet away
  - Mary – for taking her lamb to school
  - Farmer's wife – for cutting off the tails of the three blind mice
  - Jack and Jill – for breaking the bucket.
- The children produce a police report form that describes the character and gives details of his or her 'crime'. If you want to develop this further, you can hold a mock trial in the classroom, with some children taking on the roles of judge, defence, prosecution, police officers, jury members and so on.

What Should I Do?

Characters in stories often face dilemmas that raise social or moral issues. These provide an excellent opportunity to discuss character motivation in detail and address matters of social significance. Meaningful links can be made to personal, social and health education (PSHE). This activity is also sometimes called Angels and Devils.

Suitable for

KS2

Aims

- To identify social, moral and cultural issues in stories.
- To discuss how a character deals with a difficult situation.
- To relate the issue to everyday life.

Resources

- Stories that raise dilemmas (see below)

Examples of stories that raise dilemmas

- Anne Fine, *Bill's New Frock*, Methuen, 1989
- Philippa Pearce, *The Battle of Bubble and Squeak*, E.P. Dutton, 1979
- Jacqueline Wilson, *The Story of Tracy Beaker*, Doubleday, 1991

What to do

1. Discuss dilemmas in general. Ask the children what they would do if the following things happened:
   - you found a £20 note in the street
   - you saw your best friend steal something in a shop
   - you were the captain of a school team and had to decide whether to pick your best friend who was a poor player, or someone you disliked but who played well.

2. Read your chosen text to the class.

3. Choose a key event from it.

4. Hot seat the character – that is, ask one child to role play the main character for the class to ask him or her questions (see page 78 for more information).

5. Using thought and speech bubbles, ask the children, in pairs, to complete the bubbles, noting the differences between what the character *thinks* and what he or she *says*.

6. Discuss the following questions in groups.
   - What do you think should happen next?
   - What else do we need to find out before the dilemma can be resolved?
   - Are you sympathetic towards the character?

7. In groups, the children act out scenarios that address the dilemma.

Additional materials to support this activity can be viewed/downloaded at **www.pearsoned.co.uk/glynne**

Point of View

Reflecting on a story from the point of view of different characters can be very useful. Very often, a story is related from just one's character's viewpoint but a different perspective can provide the impetus for a lively discussion and help children to develop their skills of inference and deduction. Stories such as *The True Story of the 3 Little Pigs* by Jon Scieszka (Puffin, 2004) illustrate this very well – the story is told from the *wolf's* perspective!

Suitable for

KS2

Aims

- To adopt different viewpoints.
- To develop the ability to reflect on a text critically.
- To understand characters' motivation.

Resources

- Narrative texts that have been read in class novels or guided reading

What to do

1. Discuss the main events in the story and how the main character has behaved and felt.

2. Consider another character in the story. This may be the villain of the tale. For example, in *Snow White and the Seven Dwarfs*, consider events from the point of view of the (wicked) queen. A 'sympathetic' portrayal of her plight might portray her as a woman who feels that she is getting older and less beautiful. She is constantly reminded of this as she looks at the youthful Snow White. Of course, this does not

excuse her cruel command to have Snow White killed but it allows us to consider the character's motivation. It may be useful to illustrate the point of view by referring to other traditional tales. You could ask questions such as the following.

- How did Little Red Riding Hood's grandmother feel about what happened?
- What did Cinderella's father think about the sisters' behaviour?
- How did the giant feel when he met Jack at the top of the beanstalk?

3. The character could sit in the hot seat (see page 78). Cards with pre-prepared questions could be used for this or the children could devise their own.

4. Some general questions could be applied to a range of texts.

- How did you feel when the main event occurred?
- Do you like the main character in the story? If not, why not?
- Describe what happened to you at a particular point in the story.
- Why did you act as you did?
- How would you like to be remembered?

Highs and Lows

It is useful to be able to make a graphical representation of a story. This can be undertaken after reading a complete text or a chapter. The graphs can show the high and low points. Graphs can also be drawn to show the range of a character's feelings. This analysis really helps the children to gain an understanding of story structure and appeals to visual learners.

Suitable for

KS2

Aims

- To develop an understanding of story structure.
- To analyse the key points of a story.

Resources

- Texts
- Paper and pens

What to do

1. This activity can be undertaken with the whole class or in groups during guided sessions. When introducing the activity, it can be useful to take a traditional tale as an example before moving on to the specific class story.

2. Following reading a story, discuss the main events.

3. List the events in order.

4. Complete a plot profile, as illustrated in the example on page 167.

5. The vertical axis covers the range from calm to exciting and the horizontal axis the beginning of the story to the end.

Example of the technique being used to analyse Little Red Riding Hood

1. Little Red Riding Hood sets off to visit her grandmother in the woods.
2. She knocks on the door, then enters the house.
3. She goes into her grandmother's bedroom and sees the grandmother/ wolf in bed.
4. The wolf leaps out and tries to eat Little Red Riding Hood.
5. The woodcutter arrives. He cuts open the wolf and releases the grandmother.
6. The end. Calm is restored.

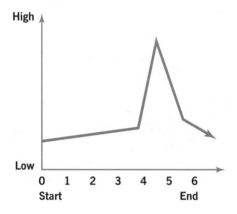

The high points of excitement are clearly when the wolf leaps out of bed and when the woodcutter arrives.

Variations

- A single chapter can be analysed in a similar way.
- Several chapters can be compared to see if the writer repeats the same format.
- Different stories can be compared in a similar way.

So You Want to Be a Princess?

Traditional tales, myths and legends are full of recurring characters – the hero, heroine and youngest child who conquers all. These activities build on children's knowledge of this format and allow them to reflect on the other common characteristics that feature in these tales.

Suitable for

KS2

Aims

- To develop the skills of inference and deduction.
- To evaluate character and justify personal views.

Resources

- A collection of familiar traditional stories, myths and legends
- List of recurring characters (see page 169)

What to do

1. These activities can be carried out independently or as a follow-up to guided or whole-class work.
2. With reference to the well-known myths or tales, introduce the idea of recurring characters – the old king, youngest son, beautiful princess, wicked witch and so on.
3. Discuss their common characteristics and make a list.
4. Identify the range of character types and consider the behaviour they display.
5. Using the list of recurring characteristics in the box as a prompt, discuss the features of a job advertisement (see page 169 for an example).

6. Model how to write a job description for the perfect princess, for example, including the skills and qualities needed.

7. Ask the children to pick a character and develop their own advertisements.

8. The adverts could be developed into Wanted! posters, which could be displayed as a gallery or collated into a large class book.

Recurring characters

- The perfect princess.
- The handsome prince.
- The wicked witch.
- The evil wizard.
- The hero who saves the day.
- The youngest son who succeeds on a quest.
- The stupid older son.
- The old king or father.
- The wicked queen.
- The hardworking mother.
- The hapless husband.
- The human (often a prince) who has been transformed into an animal.

Job advertisement

A vacancy has arisen for the post of ...
Details of education
Personal qualities needed
Skills and experience required
Application should be made to ...
Closing date ...

Variations

- Examine job advertisements from newspapers or the Internet.
- Write full job descriptions and person specifications for the character, aided by the example.

Story Skeleton

A known story can be deconstructed to reveal its bare bones – that is, its basic structure. This can then be used to retell the tale or develop a new story. This activity uses reading as a starting point, but integrates purposeful talk that may lead to a collaborative written outcome.

Suitable for

KS2

Aims

- To reflect on how stories are structured.
- To work collaboratively.
- To develop imagination.

Resources

- Copies of known texts, including traditional tales

What to do

1. Select a known story – a traditional tale or one that has been shared with the class, for example.
2. Show the children how to analyse the underlying structure of the story. Here is an example of how to do this.

   ### Cinderella

   Cinderella's father remarries and his new wife and daughters live with them. They treat Cinderella badly.

An invitation to a ball arrives, but Cinderella is not allowed to attend.

The Fairy Godmother transforms Cinderella and she goes to the ball, where she dances with the Prince, but loses her glass slipper as she leaves at midnight.

The Prince tries to find the owner of the shoe. It fits Cinderella.

The Prince and Cinderella marry and live happily ever after.

3. Model how to depersonalise the story. The story of *Cinderella* then becomes a new story.

A parent remarries and the children do not get on with the new spouse.

The children refuse to go on a long-awaited holiday with the parent, who now wishes to take the new partner. They stay at home.

They are contacted by e-mail by relatives who live in California and invite them to stay in the sunshine.

They visit their relatives where they get on so well that they are asked back every year.

4. In groups, ask the children to take the bare bones of the second account and create new stories following the basic pattern of the original story.

5. This can take the form of an oral retelling, a presentation or even a written story.

Variation

- Each group can work on a different story. Traditional tales are a good starting point.

Non-fiction activities

Read and Draw

This activity encourages children to read information carefully and locate key facts. It also provides an opportunity for them to use their phonic knowledge and sight vocabulary.

Suitable for

KS1

Aims

- To analyse simple information.
- To extract key facts.
- To practise using phonic skills and sight vocabulary.

Resources

- Simple information texts that describe a person, place or object (see page 175 for two examples)
- Highlighter pens or felt-tip pens
- Paper and pencils
- Interactive whiteboard (optional)

What to do

1. Initially, model this task so that the children understand how to locate key facts. Ensure that the text can be seen by the whole class (it could be enlarged or displayed on an interactive whiteboard).

2. First, read the text through with the children, then model how to highlight the key words. Do this with the whole class for the first two or three sentences and then ask the children to talk with their partners to decide where the key words are in the next sentence.

3. Then, model how to extract the information from the key words in order to draw what the text describes.

4. Next, give the pairs of children a similar text and ask them to read through the whole of it first before trying to locate the key facts. They could then highlight the key words or underline them with felt-tip pens. Once they have worked through all of the text, they can use the key words to help them decide what they need to draw.

Examples of simple information texts

Jack Jordan

Jack has a round head and big ears. His eyes are large and round. The left one is green and the right one is blue. Jack's nose is big and flat. His mouth is very wide. He has four top teeth. These are long and sharp. He has six bottom teeth. These are square.

The Spooky Door

The house has a big, square front door. There is one window in the top of the door. It is round and has cobwebs on it. There is a doorbell under the window. It is small and red. The letter box is in the middle of the door. It looks like a mouth. The door handle is on the left of the letter box. It looks like a bat. The door is black and the window is yellow. It shines in the dark.

Variation

- You can adapt this task so that it is a speaking and listening activity (see Barrier Games, page 34). The children work in pairs, one reads the text and the other draws the object or person or place.

Cross Me Out

Young children often find it hard to read information texts and work out which parts are important. This activity helps children to look closely at information and read for meaning.

Suitable for

KS1, can be adapted for KS2

Aims

- To make explicit links between reading and writing.
- To read for meaning.

Resources

- Short texts for children to highlight/mark (see example on page 177 and at www.pearsoned.co.uk/glynne)

What to do

1. Initially it might be a good idea to model how to use the Cross Me Out technique so the children understand what to do.

2. Use a piece of text from one of the information books in the class. Add some pieces of nonsense every few lines/sentences. The task works best if you add funny parts to the text.

3. The children work in pairs to cross out all the words that have nothing to do with the topic.

4. Once children are familiar with this technique you can move on to simple text marking/underlining (for example, looking for key words).

Example text

This text is about young babies. Cross out the bits that have nothing to do with the topic.

Newborn babies are very small. Jack sold the cow and got some magic beans. Most weigh about 3.5 kg and are only about 53 cm long. MMMMDDDDTTTT. Jack's mother was very cross. Soon after they are born babies are ready to suck milk. The milk helps the baby grow. The beanstalk grew and grew. By 3 months it weighs about 6 kg and is around 60 cm long. Jack climbed the beanstalk. It does not have any teeth yet so it cannot chew. You must chew your food.

A baby is about 8 kg and 68 cm long at 6 months old. The goose laid golden eggs. I like boiled eggs. Its body is stronger so it can sit up and play. Its little teeth are starting to come through.

This activity is adapted from an idea in *'Finding Out About Finding Out'* by Bobbie Neate (Hodder and Stoughton, 1992).

Variation

- This activity can be adapted for use with KS2. The texts do not need to be long but it is probably best to make the 'nonsense' element less obvious. This encourages the children to read the text closely so they can work out which bits are 'redundant' i.e. not needed.

Fact or Fiction?

Children need to be able to understand the difference between fact and fiction. This activity helps them to think about different sentences and which ones might be found in an information book. (See 'Is it True?', page 186 for a development of this activity at KS2).

Suitable for

Upper KS1 and lower KS2

Aims

- To make explicit links between reading and writing.
- To support children in writing non-fiction.

Resources

- A selection of sentences (fiction and non-fiction), perhaps written out on an interactive whiteboard or separate strips of card

What to do

1. Read a few of the sentences with the children. Can they work out which are facts and which are not? How can they tell? What are the clues? Are there key words that help or is it the type of language used? If you use an interactive whiteboard you could highlight some of the key words.

2. The children could then work in pairs or groups to sort the other sentences. If the sentences are written on strips of card the children could split them into two sets. Alternatively, the sentences could be written on one sheet and the children could label them fact or fiction.

3. They could then write some of their own sentences (approximately six sentences). They could look through one or two books to find some examples or devise their own. Next they could give their sentences to another pair or group to see if they can sort them.

Examples of possible sentences

Facts

Hamsters are smaller than cats.
There are seven days in a week.
Leeds is a city in the north of England.
Frogs can live in and out of water.
Spiders have eight legs.
Some trees lose their leaves in autumn.
Babies drink milk and wear nappies.
Apples and bananas are two types of fruit.
It is cold in winter.
An ostrich is the biggest bird on Earth but it cannot fly.

Fiction

Red Riding Hood knocked on the door and then went inside.
Jack grabbed the golden goose and ran as fast as he could.
Suddenly, the spaceship landed in the middle of the playground.
Mr Bear could not sleep because Mrs Bear was snoring.
She looked out of the window to wish upon a star.
In a land far away a princess looked out of a window.

Variation

- Children in KS2 could have a selection of sentences that they sort into facts/opinions. Alternatively, you could ask them to look at some 'fact' sentences and write an opinion sentence linked with each one. For example:

Fact: Hamsters are smaller than cats.
A sample opinion sentence might be: Cats are more interesting animals than hamsters.

or

Fact: Apples and bananas are two types of fruit.
Opinion: Bananas are more delicious than apples.

The Sticky Note Game

This interactive activity can be carried out during guided reading sessions and should be modelled first. The children devise their own questions, but need to consider the range of question types – inferential, deductive, literal and evaluative – and take into account that some text types offer greater opportunities for particular aspects than others. This activity can be used to reinforce work in other curriculum areas, such as science, history or geography.

Suitable for

KS2

Aims

- To develop comprehension skills.
- To develop questioning skills.
- To ask a range of questions.

Resources

- A set of guided reading information texts, not previously read
- A pack of sticky notes
- Question cards or cubes (optional)

What to do

1. Divide the guided reading group into pairs.
2. Ask each pair to work on a different text, but one that is at the same level and has not been read previously.
3. Their task is to devise two or three questions. They are to write the questions on the sticky notes and stick them on the appropriate page.

The questions should take account of the different question types and opportunities presented by the text. For example, for a text about World War II, the following types of questions would be appropriate.

- *Literal* What happened to the children from the cities during World War II?
- *Inferential* How do you think the children felt when they were evacuated?
- *Evaluative* Comment on the layout of the page and how the pictures are used.

Question cubes or cards with the key question words could be placed on the table as a reminder.

4. Ask the children to exchange their questions and books with another pair in the group and answer their questions, jotting notes on the sticky notes.
5. The books with noted answers are then passed back to the original pair.
6. Have a general discussion, focusing on the types of questions asked, how difficult it was to set the questions and whether or not they were fair rather than simply looking at the 'correct' answers.

Variations

- Once the children are familiar with the process using non-fiction texts, the essence of the questioning technique could be used in other curriculum areas.
- Focus on a chapter of a fiction text in guided reading.

What Do You Know?

This activity brings together several different strategies to support reading for information and consolidate learning. As the saying goes: 'I hear and forget, I see and remember, I do and I understand.' Children need to be involved in practical tasks so that their learning can be consolidated. This range of strategies helps children to embed their knowledge of particular concepts. They are designed to be used in a very flexible way and could be individual, paired or group tasks. They can link with non-fiction (English) or be used to support learning in other subjects.

Suitable for

KS2

Aims

- To analyse information.
- To summarise learning.

What to do

1. The children can do one or more of the following.

   - Produce a factsheet about an aspect of a topic.
   - Write five interesting facts about a chosen subject.
   - Read a text with paragraphs and give each paragraph a heading.
   - Present the information they have found as a poster.
   - Write a glossary of terms for a display.
   - Read a text and then label a drawing that accompanies it.
   - Rewrite some information for younger children.
   - Play Beat the Expert by asking each other questions about a topic they have researched.

This Is What You Do

We encounter instructional language in our everyday lives. This activity introduces the children to a wide range of 'real' texts. They examine *why* they have been written and *who* they are aimed at. The form a text takes is dictated by the reason for writing and the audience.

Audience + Purpose = Form.

Suitable for

KS1, KS2

Aims

- To introduce a wide range of instructional texts.
- To consider the audience for instructional texts.
- To consider the purpose of the text.

Resources

- A range of instructional texts – recipes, instructions from DIY products, rules for sport, rules from card and board games, instructions on food packets, manuals for appliances

What to do

For KS1

1. Link the ideas relating to instructional texts to a practical activity, such as making chocolate crispy cakes, which is easy and popular.
2. Participating in the activity enables the children to understand the need to write instructions (for reference and use in the future).
3. Model instruction writing after completing the practical sessions.

4. Work on compiling a class book of instructions. This could be added to throughout the year as the children encounter instructions across the curriculum.

5. Alternatively, small instructional books could be made, with each page focusing on a distinct element of the genre. For example:

- page 1 – Introduction – 'This book will show you how to ...'
- page 2 – list of equipment/ingredients needed
- page 3 onwards – clear, sequenced steps, perhaps accompanied by diagrams.

6. Only work with a limited range of instructional texts in KS1.

For KS2

1. This activity is a good precursor to writing instructional texts and gives a real context for the work. Give each group a small selection of instructional texts.

2. Ask them to consider:

- who the text is aimed at
- why it was written.

They can record their answers in a table such as this one.

Instructional text	Why it was written (Purpose)	Who it is aimed at (Audience)

3. Collate the findings of each group.

4. Look for similarities in terms of:

- language features – imperative, 'bossy' verbs and impersonal tone
- text layout
- use of diagrams
- sequenced steps (sometimes numbered) in time order
- materials needed.

5. Discuss the following.
   - Does the text layout serve the purpose?
   - Are the instructions easy to follow?
   - Which text is the clearest and why?

6. Make a display of the texts and encourage the class to bring in more real examples.

Is It True?

When reading newspapers and watching television, it is important to be able to distinguish between fact and opinion. These interactive activities help children to develop their ability to question what they read, hear and see.

Suitable for

KS2

Aim

- To begin to differentiate between fact and opinion with reference to media texts.

Resources

- A collection of newspaper articles from a range of newspapers
- A collection of non-fiction texts
- Access to TV and radio news programmes, such as *Newsround* (optional)
- Highlighter pens in different colours
- Sticky notes pads in different colours

What to do

1. Discuss the difference between fact and opinion:
   - fact – something *known* to be true, verifiable, a reality
   - opinion – an *unproven* belief, a personal view.
2. Share a newspaper article with the class. Discuss which facts are clearly true and which are opinion.
3. Point out modifying words that are open to interpretation – probably, might, could and possibly, for example.

4. Look for words and phrases that reinforce a point of view. Emotive language will often be used to express an opinion.

5. In an article, underline *facts* in one colour and *opinion* in another. Compare the two.

6. Divide the children into groups and ask them to look at topic books – history texts are particularly useful. Their task is to pick out what is fact and what is the author's opinion. Using two pads of sticky notes in different colours can be a helpful way for the children to indicate the pages where they have found examples of each.

Variations

- To develop this activity further, collect a range of newspapers that were printed on the same day. Compare and contrast one or two stories – how do the different papers report the same event? Which newspapers give more facts? Which express more opinions? Which newspapers use photographs to verify their stories? Does each story answer the key 'Who?', 'Where?', 'What?', 'Why?' and 'When?' questions before moving on to state an opinion?
- Watch a news bulletin on TV. Is any opinion expressed at all or is the report all factual?

Letters

Letters surround us, in either electronic (e-mail) form or on pieces of paper. They can be found in the public arena, in newspapers and magazines, or sent to a specific contact. It is therefore important that children have the experience of reading a range of letters from different contexts.

Suitable for

KS2

Aims

- To introduce a range of letters, both formal and informal.
- To introduce the conventions of letter writing.

Resources

- A collection of letters – from newspapers, e-mails, magazines, official letters, junk mail, invitations, fiction, accompanying a delivery or confirming an arrangement, personal letters (could be made up), postcards and so on

What to do

1. Divide the children into groups and give each group two letters – one formal and one informal.
2. Ask them to answer the following questions.
   - How do the letters begin?
   - How are they laid out?
   - What sort of language is used – formal or informal?
   - Is the letter typed or handwritten?

- How does the letter end?
- How do you think the person who received the letter felt?

3. Ask them what differences they notice between the formal and informal letters.

4. Take feedback from each group and extract the key features of formal and informal letters in terms of the aspects given in the table below.

	Layout	Language Is it chatty or very formal?	Tone Is the letter friendly or unfriendly?	Beginning How is the recipient addressed?	Ending How does the writer sign off?
Formal letters					
Informal letters					

5. Look at the differences between letters that are sent to a wide audience (such as letters in magazines or newspapers) and those sent to a specific person, as set out in the table below.

	Layout	Language Is it chatty or very formal?	Tone Is the letter friendly or unfriendly?	Beginning How is the recipient addressed?	Ending How does the writer sign off?
Wide audience					
Specific person					

Variation

- The children can write their own letters. Meaningful cross-curricular links can be made to history and geography, with the children applying their knowledge in order to write in role. For example, Anne Boleyn could write to Henry VIII, pleading for her life as she languishes in the Tower of London.

Additional materials to support this activity can be viewed/downloaded at **www.pearsoned.co.uk/glynne**

News Reports

Reports are clearly structured texts that are written to inform. The activities included here look at the different styles of reporting and how news reports are put together, taking account of purpose and audience.

Suitable for

KS2

Aims

- To become critical readers.
- To understand how reports are constructed.

Resources

- A range of news reports
- Highlighter pens
- Tabloid and broadsheet newspapers from the same day

What to do

The Features of Reports

1. Share a news report with the children.
2. Analyse it together in terms of the who, what, when, where and why, which should be answered in the report's introduction.
3. Using highlighter pens, investigate the text for time connectives – today, yesterday, first, next, later, then, finally and so on.
4. The children share more reports in groups.

5. Ask them to analyse these in terms of the following features:

- introduction
- facts, in chronological order
- use of time connectives
- past tense
- description of setting
- details of events
- conclusion.

Comparing Newspapers

1. Compare reports in tabloid and broadsheet newspapers from the same day. Ask the children to share their first impressions of a broadsheet and a tabloid newspaper.

2. Look in detail at one article from each type of newspaper that focuses on the same news item. Ask: are the who, what, where, when and why questions addressed in the first paragraph? Ask the children to look for differences in the language used in the different newspapers to describe the same events. Ask them the following questions:

- Does one newspaper use more adjectives than the other?
- Which newspaper uses a more formal tone?
- Is one newspaper more conversational than the other?
- Do both newspapers give the same information? Is one more detailed than the other?
- Do the accounts contain different facts?
- Does one newspaper focus on a particular aspect of the event?

3. Looking at the newspapers as a whole, the points set out in the table below can be examined in groups.

	Broadsheet	Tabloid
Audience		
Layout		
Language		
Use of photographs: number of photos subjects selected use of colour		
Adverts: if they reflect the target audience or not		

Variations

- Watch or record the television news or view Internet news sites.
- Make direct comparisons between the representation of an event in print and on screen.
  - Which gives a more considered account?
  - Which type of media conveys a truer account?
  - Which gives a more detailed account?
  - Does one type of media rely more heavily on pictures than on words?

Additional materials to support this activity can be viewed/downloaded at
www.pearsoned.co.uk/glynne

Note Making

Note making is a key skill that needs to be explicitly taught. Children should be able to identify key words and main points in a text. Generally, these key words are nouns and verbs. In essence, it is a process of deconstructing a text, breaking it down into its essential elements, then rebuilding it to show understanding.

Suitable for

KS2

Aims

- To identify key words and messages in a text.
- To note these main points in a systematic way.

Resources

- Short information texts, preferably relating to ongoing classwork
- Pictures, if using with younger children
- Mini-whiteboards
- Coloured pens, pencils or highlighters

What to do

1. It is important to model the process first with the whole class and then it needs to be revisited several times over a period.

2. With younger children, introduce the idea of note making with a picture. Ask them for one or two words that describe the picture. For example, for a picture of a steam train, key words would be *steam* and *train*.

3. Next, add three or four more key words. Continuing with the example on page 194, other key words could be *water*, *coal*, *Victorian*, *railways* and *pistons* (note that these are all nouns).

4. Ask the children to create sentences that contain the key words. They can do this in pairs, using mini-whiteboards. Each pair can take a different word. An example would be, 'The first trains were powered by coal.'

5. Model how the sentences can be put together to form a short paragraph. For example:

> *The railways developed during Victorian times. The first trains were powered by coal. As the water was heated, it drove the pistons and steam was produced.*

6. Do this several times with different texts. Ask the children to interrogate the passage to find out the who, what, where, why and how.

7. The following table can be used to demonstrate the difference between brief and fuller notes.

Key words and phrases	Fuller version
Water – heated Steam produced Pistons driven Victorian Railways developed	The railways developed during Victorian times. The first trains were powered by coal. As the water was heated, it drove the pistons and steam was produced.

Variation

- Introduce the importance of key nouns and verbs by asking the children to underline or highlight them in different colours.

Persuade Me!

We are surrounded by advertisements in both print and electronic forms. It is important that children learn how to evaluate them in terms of their impact and honesty and are aware of how they are constructed.

Suitable for

KS2

Aims

- To be able to appraise advertisements in a variety of media.
- To develop an awareness of how advertisements are put together and consider their intended impacts.

Resources

- A collection of advertisements from magazines and newspapers
- TV and radio advertisements
- Copies of tables for advert analysis to complete (see page 198)

What to do

1. Share examples of print advertisements with the class. A visualiser is useful for this. Discuss them in terms of their:
   - visual aspects:
     - headline
     - use of colour
     - choice of font
     - size of font
     - whether it features a photograph, cartoon or other kind of representation
     - background.

- language used:
  - headline
  - slogan
  - use of rhyme
  - use of alliteration
  - use of puns
  - use of metaphors and similes.

2. Discuss the advertisements in terms of whether they convey fact or opinion.

3. Discuss them in terms of any stereotyping.

4. Annotate the advert together.

5. In groups, ask the children to analyse a print advert using the tables on page 198.

6. Ask the groups to compare their findings and draw general conclusions.

7. Introduce the TV adverts. If possible, compare a TV and print advert for the same product.

8. Note the difference *sound* and *movement* make. Ask if these dimensions make the advert more effective or not. Is the sound provided by music, one or more voices, or dialogue?

9. Watch the advert with the sound turned off. Discuss the impact and effectiveness of adding sound.

10. Change a photograph into an advert.

11. Listen to some radio adverts. Note that, as there are no visual prompts, only sound and language can be used to convey the message. Look at whether or not music is used effectively. Is more than one voice used?

12. Discuss what makes an effective advert in terms of the following aspects.
    - Does it reach its target audience?
    - Is it memorable?
    - Do you recall the product or just the jingle or music?
    - Is it visually appealing?

Advert analysis

Who is the advertisement aimed at? _____

Visual features	Comments
Headline	
Use of colour	
Choice of font	
Size of font	
Photograph, cartoon, other?	
Background	

Language features	Comments
Headline	
Slogan	
Use of rhyme	
Use of alliteration	
Use of puns	
Use of metaphors and similes	

Variation

- To build on this work, the class can produce their own adverts, in print and/or film.

Additional materials to support this activity can be viewed/downloaded at **www.pearsoned.co.uk/glynne**

Biography and Autobiography

This collection of activities introduce children to the genres of autobiography and biography. They focus on making distinctions between them and distinguishing between fact, fiction and opinion.

Suitable for

KS2

Aims

- To distinguish between fact, fiction and opinion.
- To recognise the difference between 'first' and 'third' person.

Resources

- A collection of autobiographies and biographies

What to do

1. Introduce an extract from a biography and one from an autobiography to the class.

2. Ask them to identify the writer's viewpoint. Through discussion, ensure that the children understand that an autobiography is written in the *first* person and a biography is written in the *third* person. Discuss the differences between them – that autobiographies will be subjective and possibly biased, while biographies may comment on the subject's actions and offer an opinion. What effects do these differences have on readers?

3. In groups, ask the children to examine the texts for fact and opinion. Alternatively, they could work in pairs and look at the texts, highlighting fact and opinion in different colours.

4. To obtain an overview of the text and look at the chronology, ask the children to find out the following information:

- birth
- early years
- education
- adult life – the career
- later life – up to date.

5. Create a timeline. This might need to be modelled first. Ask the children to, in groups, plot these main events of the subject's life on the timeline. A timeline for William Shakespeare's life, for example, might be represented as follows.

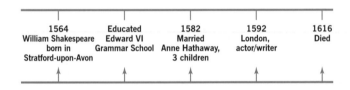

1564	Educated	1582	1592	1616
William Shakespeare born in Stratford-upon-Avon	Edward VI Grammar School	Married Anne Hathaway, 3 children	London, actor/writer	Died

Suggestions for group work

1. In pairs, ask the children to take one text and elicit the key characteristics of the subject of the book. For example, is he or she heroic, talented, clever, fearless, knowledgeable?

2. Ask the children to compare the key characteristics of the different autobiographies and biographies. These could include the following areas.

- Audience – who are the texts aimed at?
- Time covered – a whole life or part of the person's life?
- Career.
- Use of photographs.
- Style of writing – formal or informal?

3. For a biography, ask the children to focus on the tone of the text. Does the author admire the subject? How do you know?

Variation

- Use this work as a precursor to writing autobiographies. The children could produce a timeline of their own lives, plotting their own key events. This helps to give them a structure for writing their own autobiographies.

Picture It!

This practical cross-curricular activity helps children to search for and represent information in a lively, visual way. It is a useful way to introduce a topic, to visually brainstorm and categorise information.

Suitable for

KS1, KS2

Aims

- To find the key facts on a given subject from a range of books.
- To work collaboratively to brainstorm and categorise key facts.

Resources

- A collection of books on a topic
- Large (A2) sheets of paper
- Shaped cards according to the topic for younger children (rockets or planets for space, for example) or pads of sticky notes for older ones
- Felt-tip pens

What to do

1. Model the process, possibly with the whole class, using a current topic as an example.

2. Divide the class into groups.

3. Give each group a small collection of information books on a given topic – perhaps from science, history or geography.

4. Ask each group to hunt for the key facts in each book.

5. Give out the sheets of A2 paper. They can have drawn on them the outline of an aspect of the topic or older children can do this themselves.

6. The children then write the key facts they have discovered on the shaped cards or sticky notes and place them around the large drawing on their pieces of paper.

7. The groups share their findings with the whole class.

Variations

- The children move their sticky notes around to sort the facts into subgroups. For example, subgroups for space might be planets, stars and space exploration.
- Each group takes a separate aspect (subgroup) and finds out more information on that aspect of the topic. Again, for space, the result might look like this (note that Pluto is now officially regarded as a minor, dwarf planet).

Space facts

- Planets move around the Sun.
- The Sun is a star made of gas.
- The eight major planets are called Mercury, Venus, Earth, Mars, Jupiter, Saturn, Uranus, Neptune.
- The Moon is a satellite of Earth.
- Some planets have many moons.

- Moons move around planets.
- Earth is the only inhabited planet in our solar system.
- Man landed on the Moon in 1969.
- Space is black.
- Astronomy is the study of the planets and stars.

Graphic Organisers

Graphic organisers can take a variety of forms, but all help children to classify ideas and communicate more effectively. They are an excellent link between reading and writing. For younger children, they help to develop their early literacy skills. For older children, they improve their comprehension skills and help them learn how to organise ideas for writing. Graphic organisers are particularly useful for English as an additional language (EAL) children as they are able to show their understanding of subject material even if they have difficulty articulating it in spoken or written form.

Suitable for

KS1, KS2

Aims

- To analyse information.
- To organise thoughts and ideas.
- To become active learners.

Resources

- Paper, felt-tip pens, rulers
- Computers (optional)

What to do

Venn Diagram

1. Used to help children understand comparisons and contrasts in a text.
2. The format can be used when the questions ask how two things are alike and/or different.

Character Trait Web

1. Used to set out the important qualities of characters in stories and how the characters' actions reveal those qualities.

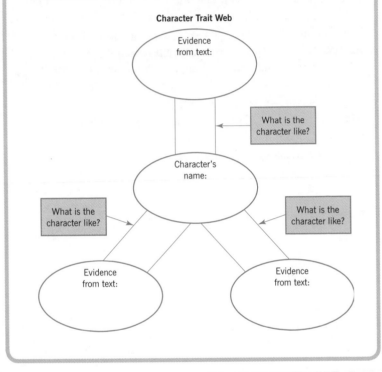

Character Trait Web

See pages 207 and 209 for other examples of graphic organisers.

Additional materials to support this activity can be viewed/downloaded at **www.pearsoned.co.uk/glynne**

Concept Map

Concept maps are tools for organising and representing knowledge. They can be used in a variety of ways, but are particularly useful for topic and cross-curricular work. They can help children sort out ideas before starting a new topic and demonstrate their new learning while studying it. They look like webs, with concepts or ideas in circles or boxes and lines between them to show the connections. Words and phrases on the lines make these links explicit.

They can be used as an Assessment for Learning (AFL) tool as they give an overview of a child's thinking and learning. The connections indicate children's understanding, pointing up any misconceptions, which can be dealt with before they become embedded.

Suitable for

KS2

Aims

- To analyse information.
- To organise thoughts and ideas.

Resources

- A3-sized paper, sticky notes or cards, pencils, felt-tip pens or concept mapping software, such as Kidspiration and 2Connect, or from the Internet

What to do

1. Introduce the idea of concept maps by modelling the process so that the children understand how they can be used. You could construct a map with the whole class that is linked to a current topic, such as habitats in science.

2. Then the children, in pairs, can talk with their partners and share their initial ideas.

3. Coming back together as a whole class, these ideas can then be used to demonstrate how to begin to create a map. It is best to identify the main concepts first and these can be written on cards or sticky notes so that they can be moved around during the construction of the map. Alternatively, you could use computer software to create the map.

4. Once you have begun the class concept map, the children can then work with their partners and start to produce their own maps. The children will probably need a whole lesson to begin to build their maps as the process takes time.

5. Later, these can be revisited and modified at the end of the topic.

Variations

- Use concept maps with English as an additional language (EAL) learners, especially those at the higher stages of language acquisition. The process of making statements by linking key words with relationship words helps to develop their language skills.
- Use concept maps with reluctant writers, as writing is not central to the activity.

KWL Chart

This is an example of a simple graphic organiser, which can be used to show prior knowledge of a topic. It can help generate children's interest in a topic and encourages them to recognise what they already know. Children often do have relevant knowledge but do not see the links in a new or different context. An important outcome is that children become more confident in creating and recording their own questions.

Suitable for

KS1, KS2

Aims

- To use prior knowledge.
- To summarise learning.

Resources

- KWL chart (see page 210), on either an interactive whiteboard or a flipchart

What to do

1. Initially, it is a good idea to model how to use the chart, particularly with younger children. Once the children understand how the chart works, they can work in pairs or individually to fill in the first two columns (see page 210).

2. The children then research a topic (this can be over several lessons) and then return to the chart to summarise what has been learned.

KWL Chart

What do I know about this topic?	What do I want to know about it?	What have I learnt about it?

Additional materials to support this activity can be viewed/downloaded at
www.pearsoned.co.uk/glynne

What Do I Want to Find Out?

 These activities are carried out before reading. They focus on the key elements of the book – chapter titles, headings and subheadings, which are used to predict what is in the text.

Suitable for

KS2

Aims

- To develop prediction skills.
- To develop skimming as a strategy.

Resources

- Information texts, such as those relating to a topic in science, history or geography

What to do

Working with One Text

1. Divide the children into pairs.
2. Ask them to focus on one chapter of a text.
3. Ask them to list the headings or subheadings (or first phrase) in each section. This will involve them skimming for key words.
4. Ask the children to consider what might be included in each section.
5. They then jot down their thoughts in a table as shown on page 213.
6. Read the text together, looking closely at the actual content and comparing this with what was predicted.

Comparing two texts

1. Compare two books on similar themes.

2. The children note their predictions on sticky notes rather than in the table and place them in the relevant parts of the book.

3. The pairs exchange their books with other pairs so that they can match their predictions with the actual text and note their findings on the sticky notes.

4. The pairs then discuss their findings with reference to the two texts.

5. As a group they compare the two texts in terms of the following, entering their conclusions in the table shown on page 213.

   - layout
   - pictures
   - detail of information
   - headings and subheadings
   - vocabulary.

Additional materials to support this activity can be viewed/downloaded at **www.pearsoned.co.uk/glynne**

Working with One Text

What do I want to find out about childhood in World War II?

Chapter and subheadings	Notes made before reading
Evacuation	
Toys	
Schools	
Games	
Abroad – childhood in Germany and Japan	

Comparing Two Texts

	Book One	Book Two
Layout		
Pictures		
Detail of information		
Headings and subheadings		
Vocabulary		

Chapter 3

Writing

Generic ideas and activities

Writing and the Role-Play Area

If planned well, a role-play area can provide an opportunity to include writing for a real purpose.

Suitable for

- Early Years, KS1

Aims

- To provide a real purpose for writing.
- To support emergent writing.

Resources

- As suggested by the theme of the role-play area

What to do

1. Role-play areas can provide the excitement and stimulation that prompt children to write naturally and with purpose. They can let their imaginations go and begin to be 'real' writers. There are many opportunities for writing within play situations (see box on page 219).

2. Ensure that there is a balance between preplanned role-play scenarios and ones that involve the children at an earlier stage. By encouraging the children to plan the area, another opportunity is provided for a real purpose for writing, such as making lists of what items are needed.

Examples of writing opportunities stimulated by role-play areas

Role play	Writing opportunities
Shoe shop, toy shop, clothes shop, music shop (CDs, DVDs).	Stock list, receipts, leaflets, instructions, price labels.
Garage, post office, dentist, doctor, vet, café.	Forms, appointments, prescriptions, order pads, message pad.
Castle, spaceship, cave, island.	Maps, signs, warnings, message in a bottle.
Stories and books, for example traditional tales, Meg and Mog	Invitations (Cinderella), shopping list (Red Riding Hood), letter to the three bears (Goldilocks), recipes for spells.

Further sources of information

- There are some wonderful resources available to support the planning of role-play areas.
  - Neil Griffiths ('inventor' of Storysacks) has produced a set of books with a wealth of ideas. See http://.storysack.com/elements/list_resource_books_packs
  - http://bigeyedowl.co.uk/roleplay.htm
  - www.nurseryactivityideas.co.uk/category/role-play-activities

Guided Writing Prompts

> 'Don't be the sage on the stage, be the guide by the side.'
> Guided writing, when used well, is a very powerful method
> for supporting children in a variety of ways. It provides you
> with opportunities to observe children as they write and
> helps develop their self-esteem.

Suitable for

KS1, KS2

Aims

- To support children's writing skills.
- To encourage children to reflect on their writing.
- To develop editing skills.

Resources

- Mini-whiteboards and pens
- Paper and pencils

What to do

1. *Before* writing, you can help children to develop skills in planning their writing, choosing prompts from the list in the 'Before writing' box (see page 221) that are appropriate for your class.

2. *During* writing, the children focus on a particular writing skill, such as writing a paragraph using notes that were made in an earlier session. Your role is to make suggestions at the point of composition, using prompts from the 'During writing' box (see page 221).

3. *After* writing, the children discuss what works well and how the writing could be improved. When working with young children, it might be

sufficient to just discuss possible improvements rather than get them to edit their writing. After all, you do not want to discourage them if they have worked hard on a piece of writing. For some prompts you could use, see the 'After writing' box on page 222.

Before writing

- What kind of text will this be?
- Who is the writing for?
- Let's say the whole sentence together.
- Where shall we begin writing?
- What is it we want to write about?
- What do we want to say?
- What ideas do we have?
- What order shall we put them in?
- How can we link the ideas together?
- What details shall we add?
- How could we start?

During writing

- What is it we want to write?
- What do we already know?
- Where will the next word go?
- How can we check it makes sense?
- Why is that word better?
- Let's reread it in a sentence and see how it sounds.
- What are the main features of this text type?
- Does it look right?
- What can we add?
- What can we leave out?
- You could try ... .

After writing

- What I liked about this was ... .
- I noticed ... .
- Which was the hardest part to get right?
- What could be improved?
- Where do you think you will put in more detail?
- What could you use to help you use alternatives to some words?
- How could you link the ideas together?

Writers' Workshop

The emphasis in this approach to the teaching of writing is on the process of writing in a number of sessions over a period of time, often culminating in making books. Children can apply the skills and strategies they have learned during shared and guided sessions.

Suitable for

KSI, KS2

Aim

- To experience all aspects of the writing process, culminating in a published outcome.

Resources

- Dictionaries, thesauruses
- Paper, range of writing tools and erasers
- Folders or draft books for ongoing work
- Author's chair
- Rhyming dictionaries for poetry (optional)
- Use of computers (optional)
- Guidance notes for response partners and drafting (optional)

What to do

Introduction

1. Writers' workshops ensure that children have dedicated time for writing. The process needs to be worked through in the course of several sessions. The emphasis is on composition initially, spelling and handwriting being addressed during the editing process. This approach to the teaching of writing recognises writing as a craft.

The writing has to be honed and revisited before generating the final product. The flow chart below sets out the different stages. It is important to model each step of the process.

Thinking and Talking

1. Introduce what it is that the children will be writing about – perhaps a story or information book for a younger child.

2. Give them time to talk over the possibilities.

Brainstorm Ideas

1. Encourage them to brainstorm ideas together and in pairs.

First Draft

1. The children start by writing their ideas down in dedicated folders or draft books.

2. Give the children time to write their first draft.

Talk and edit with Response Partner

1. The children work with a response partner, using a prompt sheet to guide them through the process (see Perfect Partners, page 227).

2. The following steps enable the children to make improvements to their writing.

   - They read their pieces aloud. This really helps make unintended repetition stand out.
   - Ask, 'How does it sound?', 'Does it make sense?'
   - They underline any words that they are not sure about.
   - They check the punctuation.
   - They work with their response partners.
   - They make the changes.

Redraft

1. Demonstrate how to redraft using some of your own writing, saying why you make the changes you do. Make it clear that this process is *not* copying out in neat!

Second Draft

1. The second draft is written.

2. This is shared with a response partner.

Publish

1. The children's work is then 'published', possibly in book form, which involves producing a copy without errors. It can be either handwritten or word processed. Here are some suggested formats:

   - zigzag
   - lift the flap
   - pop-up
   - shaped.

2. There is nothing quite like seeing your work in print and writing in special books that are then shared gives the children an immediate audience for their work. The books can be made by individuals, groups or else by the whole class.

3. Their books can be kept in a dedicated area of the classroom. You will find that they really enjoy reading one another's work.

Variation

- Use the same approach to write poetry.

Perfect Partners

Peer Marking

Working in pairs to review written work is an effective strategy that helps to develop an awareness of audience and fosters collaboration and independence. Be aware that this strategy takes some time to embed and needs to be part of the classroom culture. To introduce the process, start with sentences and paragraphs before working on completed pieces of work. Also, persevere – the children really do develop their independence and learn to apply their knowledge when working together in this way!

Suitable for

KS2

Aims

- To develop an understanding of audience.
- To develop editing skills.
- To work collaboratively.

Resources

- List of points for how to be a helpful response partner (see page 228)
- Checklist (see pages 228–9)

What to do

1. Model the process first, with another teacher or teaching assistant sharing some work and you taking the role of a critical friend. Use the checklist in the box to review his or her work.

2. Response partners can be employed at any point in the writing process, perhaps just to help review a paragraph. See the box below for how to be a helpful response partner.

3. Divide the children into pairs, taking into account individual needs.

4. Share the list for how to be a helpful response partner. (This could be copied and stuck onto card and placed on the tables or put into the children's books.)

5. Share the checklist (see box below) with the class. Each section could be mounted on separate cards.

6. The children then work on the writing in pairs, using the checklist. They can do this in a variety of ways:

- they could photocopy the work so it can be amended without disturbing the original
- they could use sticky notes to make suggestions
- they could use coloured pens and highlighters
- they could have dictionaries and thesauruses available.

How to be a helpful response partner

- Listen attentively when your partner reads his or her work.
- Thank your partner for sharing his or her work.
- Say what you liked about the work.
- Make your helpful suggestions politely.
- Use the checklist to discuss possible changes.

Checklist

Content

- Does the writing make sense?
- Is there anything missing?
- Is there anything you want to know more about?
- Is it exciting?
- Did you learn anything new?

Vocabulary

- Has the writer chosen the words carefully?
- Are there any words that you did not understand?
- Are some of the words really effective?

Techniques

- Has the writer used a range of connectives?
- Is there too much repetition?
- Does the writing have a clear beginning, middle and end?
- What about the spelling?
- Is the punctuation correct?

Change the Form

This activity involves using knowledge of genre to change the form of a text and write the story in another format, writing the story of Jack and the Beanstalk as a newspaper report, for example.

Suitable for

KS2

Aim

- To apply knowledge of genres.

Resources

- Selection of traditional tales

What to do

1. Model the process of changing genre to the children.
2. With the children working in pairs, select two text types – a story and a newspaper report, for example – and work out with them what the bare bones of the story are. For Snow White, these could be as follows.

   - Snow White is taken into the woods by the huntsman.
   - The huntsman releases her – he could not kill her.
   - Snow White stumbles across the cottage of the seven dwarves and stays with them.
   - Snow White is visited by the old witch and eats the poisoned apple.
   - As she lies in the casket, the Prince rides by.
   - As he stoops to kiss her, he dislodges the poisoned apple.
   - Snow White and the Prince marry.

3. Review what the key elements of a newspaper report are and match these with the bare bones of the story. To continue the Snow White example, this process results in the following.

- *Who*
  - Snow White, huntsman, Queen (dwarves, Prince).
- *What*
  - Snow White is taken away from her home on the Queen's orders.
  - She is spared.
  - Lives with the dwarves.
  - Eats the poisoned apple.
  - Rescued by the Prince.
- *Where*
  - 'In a land far away' – try to name a place, the forest.
- *How*
  - Cruelly (initially).
- *When*
  - Create a time and date.
- *Why*
  - Jealousy of the Queen.

4. Develop the notes into full sentences, using the third person, characteristic of a news report. For example, 'On 5 January 1207, on the orders of the Queen, Snow White was taken to Blackheart Woods by the court huntsman.'

5. Extend the report.

Variations

- Write the story or part of it as a diary entry for one of the characters.
- Create a comic strip of a story the children have recently read or of a traditional tale.
- Write the story as a letter of persuasion – the ugly sisters write to the Prince persuading him to marry one of them instead of Cinderella, for example.
- Write *Jack and the Beanstalk* as a play.
- Write instructions for the Three Little Pigs on how to build a house.

Writing Checklists

A variety of prompts to encourage children to check their writing for meaning, style, grammar and punctuation and support them in the writing process.

Suitable for

KS1, KS2

Aim

- To develop proofreading skills.

Resources

- A range of checklists displayed on posters or written on A4/A5 cards

What to do

1. Display checklists as posters in the classroom and/or provide small versions on the children's tables.
2. They can be generic ones or for specific text types (see boxes for some examples).

My Sentence Checklist (KS1)

- Does my sentence make sense?
- Have I given enough information?
- Have I used interesting words?
- Does my sentence have a capital letter and a full stop?
- Is my sentence written in the past tense?
- Is my spelling as good as it could be?

If I Get Stuck I Can ... (KS2)

- Go back to my writing plan.
- Think about who and what the writing is for.
- Talk it through with my writing partner.
- Re-read what I have written and think about what comes next.
- Say the whole sentence I am trying to write.
- Think how the writing should end.

Who Are You Writing For? (KS2)

Think about!

- Who are you writing for? **Audience**
- What are you trying to achieve? **Purpose**
- What is the best way to organise it? **Form**
- What kind of text are you writing?

Remember!

- First, work out your main ideas.
- Then, decide in which order to put them.
- Next, think how you will link them together.
- Organise your writing into paragraphs.

Grammar: Playing with language

Add the Adjective

Playing word games regularly is an enjoyable and effective way to introduce language features and an essential precursor to writing. This Victorian parlour game – sometimes known as the Parson's Cat – is an old favourite and reinforces the teaching of adjectives. It can be played with the whole class or a small group in short periods of time.

Suitable for

KS1, KS2

Aims

- To play with language.
- To reinforce the teaching of adjectives.
- To develop vocabulary.

What to do

1. Ask the children to sit in a circle.
2. The adjective that is used to describe the teacher's cat is changed by each person in the circle.
3. Younger children start by using simple adjectives, such as colours, size, shape and so on, producing sentences such as 'The teacher's cat is a *purple* cat.'
4. Older children add adjectives in alphabetical order. They can be encouraged to supply more unusual adjectives, such as the following.
   - First participant: 'The teacher's cat is an *admirable* cat.'
   - Second participant: 'The teacher's cat is a *bashful* cat.'
   - Third participant: 'The teacher's cat is a *capable* cat.'

5. The game can be developed by adding a name for the cat.

- The teacher's cat is an admirable cat *called Alfred*.
- The teacher's cat is a bashful cat *called Billy*.
- The teacher's cat is a capable cat *called Claire*.

6. The game does not have to be played alphabetically.

7. When the children become proficient, they can challenge each other to use more unusual adjectives.

Variations

- The children research a range of unusual adjectives using dictionaries. Working in pairs, each pair contributes up to five adjectives. They can also be alert for adjectives as they read.
- Create an adjective tree. New and unusual adjectives are written on a leaf and these are placed on a branch of the adjective tree.

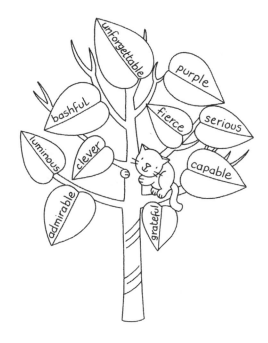

- Younger children can make a book illustrating the different cats.
- It can be helpful to have a selection of adjectives written on cards for children to use if they cannot think of a word to contribute. Alternatively, the child can 'pass'.

Guess My Move - Verbs and Adverts

This activity is an enjoyable way to reinforce work on verbs and adverbs and help extend vocabulary. The game can be played in spare slots of time as well as during dedicated literacy sessions.

Suitable for

KS1, KS2

Aims

- To develop work on verbs and adverbs.
- To broaden vocabulary.

Resources

- Sets of verb and adverb cards (see boxes on pages 240 and 241), using one colour for verbs, another for adverbs

What to do

1. Before starting the game, sort the cards into two piles and check that the verbs match the adverbs to some degree, so the mime is feasible.

2. Select one child from the class or group.

3. Ask him or her to pick two cards – one verb card and one adverb card – from the top of each pile and not show them to anyone.

4. Next, he or she mimes what is on the cards to the rest of the class – perhaps 'hop' (verb) 'cautiously' (adverb).

5. The rest of the class must guess *what* he or she is miming – the verb – and *how* he or she is moving – the adverb. They must guess the *verb* first. They will do this quite quickly – after all, it's obvious when someone is hopping! Guessing the adverb, though, presents more of a challenge, but all the suggestions and questioning helps to develop vocabulary.

6. The child who guesses the correct adverb takes his or her turn at miming and chooses two cards.

Variation

- Add an oral dimension. Ask the children to select an adverb card and answer their name at registration in the manner of the adverb – quietly, carefully, slyly, enthusiastically, for example.

Some examples of verbs and adverbs you could use

Verbs

Run, hop, skip, jump, crawl, yawn, sing, write, draw, sleep, climb, walk, smile, frown.

Adverbs

Carefully, cautiously, gracefully, unkindly, fiercely, cleverly, slowly, quickly, proudly, defiantly, awkwardly, pleasantly, charmingly.

Abstract or Concrete?

What's that Noun?

> This activity helps to reinforce the teaching of different types of nouns.

Suitable for

KS2

Aim

- To give practice at categorising nouns in an interactive and engaging way.

Resources

- Noun grid – this can be printed from the website **www.pearsoned.co.uk/ glynne**. It is useful if this can be reproduced onto A3 card or paper

Common nouns	Proper nouns	Collective nouns	Abstract nouns

- Collection of noun cards – a selection can be found at **www.pearsoned.co.uk/ glynne**. This includes the following:

Common nouns	Proper nouns	Collective nouns	Abstract nouns
farm	France	gaggle	pride
man	Mississippi	gang	happiness
queen	Lord Smith-Jones	flock	awe
fork	Princess Diana	pack	kindness
car	Colonel Blimp	swarm	jealousy
boy	James	team	hope
sea	Middlesex	colony	deceit
dog		herd	anger
desk		crowd	fear
table		troupe	hatred
horse		gang	joy
country		galaxy	
house			

What to do

1. This activity can be played in groups or as part of a guided writing session.

2. A group is given a noun grid (as on page 242) and a collection of noun cards.

3. The children put the nouns into the appropriate place on the grid.

4. A discussion may ensue about the categorisation.

Note: You may find that the common and proper noun sections are completed easily. However, the collective and particularly the abstract nouns may present more of a challenge.

Developing further - understanding abstract nouns

- Point out that abstract nouns are intangible (cannot be directly touched or seen) and are often associated with an emotion – sadness, hate, anger, joy etc.
- Place the abstract nouns face down. Invite a child to select one of the cards.
- The child mimes the noun, focusing on facial expression and body language. The rest of the group guesses the noun. The child who guesses correctly takes the next turn at selecting the card and miming the abstract noun.
- Follow this up by inviting the children to identify abstract nouns in their reading. Useful discussions can ensue in guided reading sessions about the use of the abstract noun and the effect on the reader.

Making the Connection - Connectives

Connectives have a key function in creating complex sentences and cohesive texts. This practical activity familiarises children with a range of connectives.

Suitable for

KS2

Aims

- To understand the function of connectives.
- To use a range of connectives.

Resources

- Sentence strips
- Connectives on cards (see page 245)
- Paper and pens

What to do

Initial game - Does This Make Sense?

1. The aim of this game is to find an appropriate connective.

2. In small groups, perhaps during guided writing, ask each child to write a simple sentence. You can use some sentence starters if the children need support.

3. Ask the children to pass their sentences to those next to them and then for those children, in turn, to read them out and take a connective card from the pile.

4. They each decide whether or not the words make sense when added onto the ends of their sentences. If they *do* fit, they complete the sentences. For example, if the sentence is 'She was pleased with her

new dress' and the connective picked is 'however', the result could be 'She was pleased with her new dress, however she hoped no one else had that style as she wanted to feel special.' If a word does *not* fit, the group discusses why that is the case.

Categorising Connectives

1. Ask the children to sort the connectives cards by type or function – you may need to model this first.
2. Ask them to think about whether each one is a connective of time, cause, addition or opposition.

Examples of connectives

however	therefore	then
because	additionally	before
so	just	in conclusion
as	later	although
on the other hand	earlier	since
furthermore	but	except
nevertheless	as soon as	unless
also	in the meantime	rather
as well as	immediately	even if

Additional materials to support this activity can be viewed/downloaded at **www.pearsoned.co.uk/glynne**

Connective Consequences

Connectives are key to producing coherent and varied writing. This engaging interactive game will help children to apply and consolidate the teaching of connectives.

Suitable for

KS2

Aims

- To reinforce the teaching of connectives.
- To raise awareness of the effect of selecting the appropriate connective when writing.

Resources

- Paper and pencils
- Lists of connectives (optional) – see **www.pearsoned.co.uk/glynne**
- Examples of simple sentences (optional)

What to do

1. Children are grouped into threes. This is played as Consequences.
2. The first child writes a simple sentence, for example, *The boy ran across the road*, and folds over the paper.
3. He or she passes the paper to the next child who adds a connective, for example, *therefore,* and folds over the paper.
4. The third child writes another simple sentence, for example, *It is raining today*.

5. The paper is unfolded to reveal the complete text. This may result in some unusual pieces and some interesting discussion.

   - Does it make sense?
   - If not, would it help to change the connective?
   - Is there any connection at all between the first and last sentence?
   - Would it help to change the tense?

   In the example given the final text would have read: *The boy ran across the road* **therefore** *it is raining today*. Clearly this does not make sense. A discussion might ensue – perhaps replace *therefore* with **and**. *The boy ran across the road* **and** *it is raining today* – this makes sense!

   The point of the discussion would be to elicit **why** the original sentence is not plausible and raise awareness of precise choice of words.

6. Carry on playing the game – sometimes it is just fun to see what happens.

Pick a Preposition

> Prepositions are words that show the connections between things – for example, *The cat sat on the mat*. There are a limited number (about 150) of prepositions in the English language. This activity encourages children to practise creating sentences that include prepositions.

Suitable for

KS2

Aim

- To reinforce and apply the teaching of prepositions.

Resources

- Preposition cards – see page 249 and **www.pearsoned.co.uk/glynne**
- Noun cards – see page 250 and **www.pearsoned.co.uk/glynne**. These could be random nouns or themed and related to a current class project

Note: Print the noun and preposition cards in different colours.

What to do

This is a group activity. It can be played orally initially and/or in the written format as described below. The aim is to create an interesting sentence using the cards as a prompt.

1. Place the preposition and noun cards in the centre of the table.
2. Each child takes a preposition card and a noun card.
3. He or she has to create a sentence that incorporates both selected words. They are written on a whiteboard. For example, ***below*** and ***sea*** – *Fish live **below** the **sea*** may be written as a simple sentence.

4. Pass the whiteboard to the next child and ask him or her to add to the sentence. A possible sentence might be: *The shimmering rainbow fish live **below** the tropical **sea**.*

Prepositions

about	down	on top of
above	during	outside
across	except	over
against	for	past
along	from	since
among	in	through
at	in front of	to
before	into	towards
behind	like	under
below	near	until
beneath	of	up
beside	off	with
between	on	within
by	onto	without

Nouns: starter suggestions for cards

cat	sea	stone tower	fort
dog	jungle	dark cave	spaceship
horse	mountain	ancient castle	tall ship
monkey	sharp rocks	huge mansion	football
man	gnarled stick	house	computer
woman	ancient tree	remote hut	mobile phone
old lady	table	famous restaurant	magic carpet
old man	golden chair	tunnel	curved knife
boy	book	garden	fur coat
girl	street	palace	cobweb

Variation

- Use prepositions to create a class poem. This will help the children to internalise the function of prepositions and can result in some effective writing.

  Here's an example:

  Behind *the wall they discovered a magical garden*

  In front of *the garden stood a fountain of delights*

  Beyond *the fountain was a tunnel of surprises*

  Beneath *the tunnel the monster roared!*

Consequences - Reinforcing Word Classes

This activity reinforces the teaching of word classes in an entertaining and enjoyable way. Model it first perhaps during a guided writing session.

Suitable for

KS2

Aims

- To reinforce the teaching of word classes.
- To develop an awareness of sentence structure.

Resources

- Pens or pencils
- Copies of grid (see page 252)

What to do

1. Divide the children into small groups to play this game, which is like Consequences.
2. Using the grid on page 252, each child adds a word under the first heading. The paper is passed around the group with the next child adding a word under the next heading and so on.
3. Share the final sentences that have been made – there may be some amusing results!
4. Decide whether the sentences are sense or nonsense (see the example on page 252).
5. Amend the sentences so that they make sense.

Grid

	Adjective	Noun	Verb	Adverb	Preposition		Noun
The						at/the	
The						at/the	
The						at/the	

Example of a completed row

	Adjective	Noun	Verb	Adverb	Preposition		Noun
The	mischievous	monkey	jumped	amazingly	towards	the	Moon

The above sentence makes sense (even though it's unrealistic!)

Variations

- Make human sentences. This is appropriate for younger children as it introduces the notion that different words have different functions. Each child holds up a card with one word from a given sentence. The child who holds the adverb walks from one position in the sentence to another. This provides an opportunity to discuss the different effects that can be created, as can be seen in the sentences, 'She walked into the room *cautiously*' and '*Cautiously*, she walked into the room.' What difference does moving 'cautiously' make?
- Cards for each word class can be used instead of the grid. It is helpful to use a different colour for each word class – red for adjectives, blue for verbs for example. Lay the cards for each word class out, face down in the same order as the columns in the grid, then ask each child to turn a card over. Place the cards next to each other in order and discuss the final sentence that has been made. Does it make sense?

- Use a word class die. Write the names of the six word classes from the grid on page 252 on the blank faces of a die. Each child rolls the die and provides a word from the word class shown by the die. After a few turns, the children build up a collective sentence that makes sense.

Additional materials to support this activity can be viewed/downloaded at **www.pearsoned.co.uk/glynne**

Phrases to Sentences

A group of words that does not make complete sense by itself is a phrase. Words need to be added to it in order to make complete sense. This activity gives the children practice at creating meaningful sentences.

Suitable for

KS2

Aims

- To distinguish between phrases and sentences.
- To reinforce the notion of the sentence.

Resources

- Phrase cards – see page 255 and available at **www.pearsoned.co.uk/glynne**

What to do

1. The children work in a group. Place the phrase cards in the centre of the table.
2. Each child in turn takes a phrase card. They have to turn the phrase into a sentence by adding a few words at the beginning or end of the phrase accordingly.
3. If a rather 'boring' sentence is offered, other members of the group can challenge the child. However, they have to provide a more interesting sentence.
4. Add an extra element by 'Beating the Clock' and supplying the rest of the words in a given time.

Phrase cards

Add a few words to the **beginning** to create sentences.

... through the snow.
... into the water.
... yesterday evening.
... under the trees.
... are great friends.
... is burning brightly.
... has lost his football.
... are being mended.
... is sitting in the living room.

Phrase cards

Add a few words at the **end** to create sentences.

The horse was pulling ...
The candles lit up ...
The flood damaged ...
On the sands ...
Down the river ...
Into the air ...
With a roar of rage ...
Lying on the table ...
Two dogs were walking ...

What's in a Sentence?

This activity helps children to construct sentences and begin to be aware of types of words – word classes – and how they change the meaning of a sentence. Involving children in this type of activity supports and improves their writing.

Suitable for

- KS1, for a KS2 development, see Consequences, page 251)

Aims

- To develop an awareness of sentence structure.
- To experiment with creating sentences.

Resources

- A range of starter sentences, on cards or displayed on an interactive whiteboard (see page 258)
- Starter lists of adjectives, nouns and verbs, using different colours of card or writing them in different colours on a whiteboard

What to do

1. Write or type a sample sentence – the brown dog jumped over the bucket, for example.

2. Read the sentence with the children and talk about the different words. It is probably best to focus on one word class initially, such as adjectives, and not use technical vocabulary with very young children.

3. Talk about the word that comes before 'dog', asking, 'What does it tell us about the dog?' and 'What other word could we put there instead?'

You could use one of the words from the list or see if the children can think of a word.

4. Try out some of the children's suggestions and talk with them about how the sentence changes.

5. Next, focus on the verb and ask the children similar questions, such as 'What does it tell us about the dog?' and so on.

6. With the children in pairs, ask them to talk with their partners to see if they can think of a different word. Some children find this harder than thinking of adjectives so you may have to use some of the words from your list.

7. If the children are able to, focus next on the last word in the sentence. Some children may get confused by lots of changes, so use your judgement and see if it is best initially to leave this word unchanged.

8. Give each pair of children different starter sentences and some small sets of word cards. You can decide which words you want them to focus on – just adjectives, or adjectives and verbs. The children can then experiment with the words and see how many different sentences they can make.

9. An extra challenge you can give the children is to ask them, for example, 'What is the funniest sentence you can make?'

Variations

- Put the words on large cards and then ask the children to make human sentences (see page 258). This is often an easier method for young children as they can see very clearly what happens to the sentence when some words are changed.
- Use the sentences the children create to make flip books. These can be revisited to reinforce and extend the activity.

Examples of starter sentences for Year 1

These examples ask children to experiment with just the nouns, but you could adapt them so that the children focus on adjectives instead.

	Adjective	Noun	Verb			Noun
The	brown	dog	jumped	over	the	bucket
The	grey	rabbit	hopped	under	the	
The	beautiful		ran	around	the	
The	huge		hid	behind	the	
The	tiny		fell	down	the	

Starter sentences for Year 2

This version has fewer elements completed than the table for Year 1, so the children focus particularly on varying the adjectives and verbs. As with the Year 1 example, you can adapt it to suit your purposes. Note that you always need to provide the prepositions as the children find it difficult to think of these for themselves.

	Adjective	Noun	Verb			Noun
The	brown	dog	jumped	over	the	bucket
The	small	rabbit		under	the	house
The				around	the	car
The				behind	the	shed
The				down	the	hole

Additional materials to support this activity can be viewed/downloaded at
www.pearsoned.co.uk/glynne

Name that Paragraph

Children do find it difficult to organise their writing into paragraphs. This practical activity will give them an opportunity to explore paragraph order.

Suitable for

KS2

Aim

● To order texts into sequential paragraphs.

Resources

● Texts – non-fiction or narrative (an example is given on page 260 and is available on the accompanying website **www.pearsoned.co.uk/glynne**)

What to do

Note: Demonstrate this initially in a shared or guided session. This can be done electronically or using paper.

1. Read a piece of jumbled text.
2. Re-read it a paragraph at a time and create a heading for each paragraph.
3. Using either the cut and paste facility on a computer (or paper and scissors) reorder the text to make coherent sense.
4. Re-read the text – does it flow and is there a logical progression?

Text Example

This can be cut up and re-arranged so it becomes a jumbled text.

School Journey

Last January Mrs Jones announced that in April the class would have the chance to go on a week's trip to Adventure Land. Everyone was thrilled, excited and a little apprehensive – they'd heard from last year's group that they'd be expected to climb rocks, canoe along a fast-flowing river and swim in the ice-cold sea!

First, they had to take the letter home and find out if their parents would allow them to go. Permission letters had to be received before names were added to the list. Most people were lucky enough to be going.

Next, a list of clothing and equipment was given out. This included rucksacks (no suitcases), heavy walking boots and waterproofs – waterproof trousers, waterproof jackets and waterproof hats. Were they expecting rain? Swimsuits and casual clothes were also mentioned as well as the obvious things like pyjamas, toothbrush and soap! There would be a disco as a special treat so it was suggested that they bring along one fancy outfit – a bit of a contrast to all the outdoor hiking gear!

After that, time seemed to stand still for about three months. Every Monday morning they handed over their weekly payments to Mrs Jones and she ticked them off on the (electronic) register – some kind of spreadsheet that could automatically work out how much they still had to contribute. They were all getting really excited and Mrs Jones kept on telling them to calm down and concentrate. The countdown seemed eternal!

February and March passed quite quickly. An endless round of work, work, work with the occasional break for a bit of music or PE. Well, it certainly seemed like that. They did masses of project work about the village they'd be visiting, which was by the sea in Cornwall and used to be run by smugglers – they all hoped that they'd still be there – how cool would that be? (Not sure Mrs Jones would have been too pleased though!)

At last April arrived. The sun decided to make a welcome appearance – perhaps they wouldn't need all those waterproofs after all? Nearly there! They spent what seemed like hours checking and double checking their kit lists. They'd been told to be responsible and not just leave it to their parents – after all, they would not be there. For most of them it would be their first time away from home – both exciting and scary.

On 12 April at 7.00 am they met up bleary-eyed but very excited in the playground at school. They loaded their rucksacks into the hold, clambered on board the gleaming coach and found their seats. Mrs Jones and the other teachers kept walking up and down the coach checking and double checking that they were all there. As the coach pulled out of the school drive the adventure could begin.

Question or Statement?

This activity will help the children to differentiate between statements and questions.

Suitable for

KS2

Aim

- To consolidate understanding of the difference between statements and questions.

Resources

- A collection of sentences to include statements and questions (see **www. pearsoned.co.uk/glynne**).
- Egg timer – optional

What to do

1. Print the sentences out onto individual cards (adding some more of your own if you wish). You may choose to print the statements and questions onto different coloured card.

2. In pairs or groups the children match the statement to the corresponding question, for example, *'When is Tom's birthday?'* (question) matches *'Tom's birthday is in November'* (statement).

3. An element of competition can be introduced if the activity is timed against the clock. How quickly can the children match the statement to the question?

4. Develop this further by splitting the children into pairs and asking each pair to compose a question. At a given signal they pass their question to another pair who write the equivalent statement. This can be done on mini-whiteboards. It's more fun if this is timed – an egg timer works well.

Example statements and questions

Examples could include the following, which are reproduced at
www.pearsoned.co.uk/glynne

Statements – tell people things and account for most spoken and written
sentences.

Questions – ask something, often using question words – when, why,
what, where, how? Don't forget to add the question mark.

Statement	Question
Jane enjoys painting.	Does Jane enjoy painting?
The football team won their match today.	Did the football team win their match today?
Their school uniform is navy blue.	What colour is their school uniform?
Mrs Jones went to the shops at lunchtime.	Where did Mrs Jones go at lunchtime?
The castle overlooked the river.	What did the castle overlook?
Henry VIII had six wives.	How many wives did Henry VIII have?
Tom's birthday is in November.	When is Tom's birthday?
There are 30 children in our class.	How many children are there in our class?
I would like to fly into space.	Would you like to fly into space?
I was given a computer for Christmas.	What were you given for Christmas?
I would like to go to the cinema on Wednesday with Uncle Bill.	Would you like to go to the cinema on Wednesday with Uncle Bill?
My favourite colour is red.	What is your favourite colour?

Variations

- Develop the activity further by producing four different types of sentence – statement, question, command and exclamation. Ask the children to compose sentences under each heading. Taking a theme (such as the current project) will result in a more coherent set of sentences.
- Collect texts that give examples of statement, command, question and exclamatory sentences. Newspapers are a useful source. Examine the variety of sentences types that predominate in different newspapers – for example, compare tabloids and broadsheets.

Sentence Activities

It can be difficult to explain what a sentence is to young children. These strategies can help to develop this concept and also support the children in recognising when they have written a sentence.

Suitable for

KS1

Aim

- To develop the concept of a sentence.

Resources

- Flipchart or whiteboard
- Interactive whiteboard (optional)
- Sentence or word strips

What to do

Make a Sentence

1. Write out some sentences from a well-known book or story, such as the text you are using for shared reading.

2. Cut each sentence in half and give the halves to different pairs of children.

3. They then read their incomplete sentence and see if they can find the pair of children who have the other half of their sentence.

4. Once the halves are together, they check that the sentence makes sense and it has a capital letter and full stop.

5. Some of the children can then read out their sentences to the rest of the class.

Match the Sentence

1. In pairs, give the children several sentence strips that have been cut in half.

2. Can they match the sentences? Do they make sense?

I Can Make a Rainbow

1. During shared writing, use a different colour for each sentence. Make sure that some of the sentences continue from one line to the next. Point out to the children how the different colours show where one sentence ends and another begins.

2. A way to develop this activity is to get the children to use two coloured pens when doing paired writing on small whiteboards. Alternatively, they could use a computer and change the colour of the font for each sentence.

Does it Sound Right?

1. In a whole-class session, write a short story, but with the capital letters and full stops in the wrong places. Write it on a flipchart or whiteboard or you could use a computer and then display the text on an interactive whiteboard.

2. Read the story with the children, asking, 'Does it sound right?'

> The dog was sitting.
>
> By the fire he was getting.
>
> Very hot he went into.
>
> The kitchen and had.
>
> A drink he then sat.
>
> In his basket

3. Involve the children in editing the text, putting the punctuation in the right places.

Stretch a Sentence

Research has shown that sentence manipulation can play an important part in the development of writers. This activity helps children to experiment with sentences and encourages them to include more information.

Suitable for

KS1, can be adapted for KS2

Aims

- To experiment with sentences.
- To expand a sentence by adding extra information.

Resources

- A selection of simple starter sentences – on cards or on an interactive whiteboard (see page 268)
- Paper and coloured pens or mini-whiteboards

What to do

1. Start with a simple sentence, such as 'The cat sat on the mat.'
2. Model how to stretch the sentence by answering the questions *Who, Where, When, Why, How*? For example, for the above sentence, the following answers could be generated.
   - Who? Sid, the black cat, sat on the mat.
   - Where? Sid, the black cat, sat on the mat in the kitchen.
   - When? Sid, the black cat, sat on the mat in the kitchen early in the morning.
   - Why? Sid, the black cat, sat on the mat in the kitchen early in the morning because he was hungry.
   - How? Sid, the black cat, sat impatiently on the mat in the kitchen early in the morning because he was hungry.

3. Alternatively, model the answers to just one or two questions and then ask the children to think of some ideas. When writing the extra pieces of information that stretch the sentence, using a different-coloured pen for each part makes the additions clearer to the children.

4. Initially this is a whole-class activity, but, once the children have become familiar with the concept, they can then work in pairs to stretch different sentences by themselves.

5. The children could answer just two or three questions rather than all five. They could stretch the sentences orally before writing them.

Variations

- For KS2 children, start to play around with each expanded sentence to see if it could be improved further. Suggest, for example, that the words could be moved around or the sentence could be split up. For example, using the stretched sentence on page 267 part of it could be moved to the beginning.

  Early in the morning Sid, the black cat, sat impatiently on the mat in the kitchen because he was hungry.

- Alternatively, the adverb could be moved and the long sentence could be divided into two new ones.

  Impatiently, Sid, the black cat, sat on the mat in the kitchen. It was early in the morning and he was hungry.

- Talk with the children about the different sentences and which format produces the best effect.

Some sample starter sentences

- They went on holiday.
- He went into the forest.
- They went to the beach.
- She went on the train.
- She killed the monster.
- He was in the barn.
- She flew in the air.

Present to Past

Verb Tenses

Children can become confused by verb tense.
Inconsistency of tenses is commonly found in written work.
This activity raises awareness of tense and highlights the
effect that changing tense can have on the reader.

Suitable for

KS2

Aims

- To raise awareness of the importance of tense.
- To practise at changing tense and analysing the effect.

Resources

- Text – see page 270 and **www.pearsoned.co.uk/glynne**
- Highlighter pens

What to do

1. Read the passage on page 270 – it is written in the present tense.
2. Working in pairs, one child reads the passage aloud to their partner.
3. Using highlighter pens they identify all the verbs.
4. In pairs they change the verbs from present tense to past tense. The passage is reproduced in double spacing to facilitate this.
5. Compare the effect of the two versions by reading the edited/amended passage aloud.
6. Discuss the differences in terms of tone and how it affects the reader.

Note: This activity can be completed electronically as an alternative.

Past into Present

It's the middle of the afternoon and I'm walking along the street minding my own business. This strange-looking woman comes up to me. She's wearing a long red skirt, green shoes and a purple shawl that clashes with the skirt. Her long blonde hair hangs in limp clumps and on the top of her head sits a floppy black hat.

I try to cross the road and get out of her way when she catches up with me.

'Excuse me,' she says very politely, 'do you know the way to the station? I'm supposed to be meeting my niece and I think I'm rather late.'

'Oh!' I say, taken aback by her polite but friendly manner. 'It's across the road and the second on the left.'

'Thank you, you are most kind,' she replies and gives me a warm smile. Then she turns on the heel of her green pointed shoe and walks off in the direction of the station.

They say 'you can't judge a book by its cover' and you know, they may be right!

Say It Right!

Using Standard English

> Children are sometimes confused by non-standard forms of English. This activity gives them an opportunity to act as proofreaders and write in standard form.

Suitable for

KS2

Aim

- To raise awareness of non-standard and standard English.

Resources

- The text on page 273 (also available at **www.pearsoned.co.uk/glynne**)

What to do

1. The children work in pairs.
2. Using the text, which is in the form of a playscript, they each take a role.
3. They read the text aloud in pairs as a script.
4. They discuss the non-standard forms that are used and identify the errors specifically.
5. They correct the mistakes using Standard English.
6. Re-read the passage aloud with the children.
7. Discuss the differences and why the original does not work well. The discussion will identify incorrect use of tense, over-use of superlatives and redundant words.

Say It Right

Two young girls, Susie and Jane, are having a conversation in the playground.

Susie: Your new bike is more nicer than mine.

Jane: Well, I just got it for my lastest birthday. But you've got the bestest scooter in the school – it's all shiny and clean.

Susie: Have you seen Mr Jones's new jacket? I think it's the horriblest I've ever seen – all green with navy stripes!

Jane: I agree, it's one of the worstest I've seen. I think he gotted it from that shop at the end of the street. I seed it in the window.

Susie: Mr Jones usually wears nice clothes. He done wrong with that jacket.

Jane: Did you get your homework done last night?

Susie: Yes and I gived it in this morning as I was stood by the door.

Jane: Did you done it right?

Susie: I'm not sure. I often get words mixed up. I think I need to practise to get them right!

Jane: Me too.

Spelling

Spell Away!

Regular routines for checking and practising spelling need to be established. The following strategies are effective for helping children to take responsibility for their spelling and address their personal spelling needs.

Suitable for

KS1, KS2

Aims

- To improve spelling.
- To develop an awareness of personal spelling issues.
- To integrate spelling into everyday classroom routines.

Resources

- Some scrap paper, exercise books, mini-whiteboards
- Dictionaries

What to do

General strategies

Response Partners

1. Having a response partner (see page 227) encourages children to review their work and pick out those words that they frequently spell incorrectly.

2. They can create a personal 'tricky' words list.

3. They can test each other regularly – it takes time to embed correct spellings!

Have a Go Pads

1. This approach can be modelled, acknowledging that we *all* make mistakes! It takes time and practise to spell well.

2. Have scrap paper available so that the children can try out spellings and use mini-whiteboards so that errors can be erased immediately.

3. Encourage the children to underline any words that they think are incorrect.

4. Show them that they can use a 'have a go pad' or mini-whiteboard to try out a piece of writing first.

5. The children then check their writing with you.

6. They then rewrite the words that have errors in them.

7. They ask another child to check these words.

8. They then check the words in a dictionary.

Spelling Journals

1. Spelling journals can be used to help with children's individual needs and are an integral part of the writing process.

2. Use spelling journals with the children to:

   - make a log of tricky words
   - keep a record of effective words that can be used in writing
   - collect words on specific topics
   - build up words that are spelt successfully
   - note any helpful strategies, such as mnemonics
   - collect word families
   - list useful rhymes.

Specific strategies

Mnemonics

1. Mnemonics help us to remember something tricky. The initial letter of each word in a memorable sentence is used to spell out a tricky word or an unforgettable idea is attached to a word.

2. Ask the children to make up their own mnemonics as well as using some old favourites, such as the following.

- Billy Eats Custard And Uncle Sells Eggs helps us to write *because*.
- Rhythm Helps Your Two Hips Move help us to remember how to write *rhythm*.
- To remember how many 'C's there are in ne**ces**sary, think of it as having one 'collar' and two 'sleeves'.

Word Detective

1. Ask the children to pretend that they're detectives, looking for words hiding within other words.

2. You could use the following examples.

- Sepa**rat**e – can you see the rat?
- W**hen** – can you find the hen? (They frequently omit the 'h'.)
- All the following words contain 'here' and refer to 'place':
- – **here**
- – w**here**
- – t**here** – (this also helps to stop the confusion with '**their**', for which you can ask, 'Can you see *heir* in *their*?').

Spell Well

The interactive activities included here help develop an awareness of words from the early years.

Suitable for

KS1

Aims

- To develop an awareness of how words look.
- To develop phonological awareness.

Resources

- Paper and pencils
- Alphabet and noun prompt cards, such as picture cards
- Pictures of familiar settings or objects (optional)

What to do

Word Families

1. Here are a few ideas for activities related to word families.
    - Build up word families – at, ot, or, ee, ea, oa.
    - Set the children a challenge – which group can find the most words in five minutes, for example.
    - Display the words in books or as posters in the class.
    - Create class and individual books of memorable word families. For example, the 'og' family:

        M**og** the fr**og**

        met a d**og**

        jumped over a l**og**

        got stuck in a b**og**

Rhyming sentences

1. The aim of this game is to add a rhyming word. Have noun prompt cards handy.

2. Put the pile of noun prompt cards face down on the table, then ask a child to turn over a card and add a rhyme. For example:

   - in the *park* it is *dark*
   - in the *school* there is a *jewel*
   - in the *house* there is a *mouse*.

Word Ladders

1. The children are in pairs. Begin with the first child thinking of a word, such as 'car'.

2. The second child changes one letter to make a new word, so 'car' becomes 'cat', for example.

3. The first child then does the same thing to make another new word – changing 'cat to 'can', for instance.

4. This continues back and forth – 'can' becoming 'man' and so on.

Follow-on Words

1. The children take turns making up words that begin with the last letter of the previous word – girl, lake, elephant, trips, sea, animal, for example.

Pelmanism

1. Using the set of alphabet cards, this game focuses on initial sounds.

2. Ask a child to turn over a card and say the name of the letter, the sound the letter makes and a word beginning with that letter.

Hot Potato

This is a simple activity to help children consolidate their knowledge of particular phonemes/words, for example consonant clusters, rhyming words etc.

Suitable for

KS1, could be adapted for KS2 – see page 282)

Aims

- To develop phonological awareness.
- To support word knowledge.

Resources

- A bean bag or ball

What to do

1. This game can be used to reinforce the learning of sets of phonemes. For example, after working on some consonant clusters with the children ask them to sit in a circle. One person starts (initially this will need to be modelled but once the children are familiar with the activity they can take turns to start the game).

2. You could provide the first word or the child could think of his or her own. For example, for the consonant cluster 'pl', the first word could be 'play'. The first person says the word then throws the bean bag (or ball) to another child who has to say a word that starts with the same consonant cluster.

3. This continues until someone says 'All change'. When this happens the next person has to think of a different consonant cluster and then the game continues as before.

Variations

- This activity can be adapted for Key Stage 2 by using more complex spelling patterns, for example, prefixes, suffixes etc.
- You could play Roll the Ball (a soft sponge ball works well) with Foundation/ Y1 children. The aim is to continue a rhyming string. As you roll the ball across the circle say a word from a rhyming family, for example, 'coat'. The child who receives the ball has to add a word that rhymes, for example 'boat'. Continue rolling the ball across the circle until everyone has had a go or until you or they can't think of any more words. You can then start a new rhyming string.

It's Raining Words!

These two simple activities help children to consolidate their phonic and spelling knowledge.

Suitable for

KS1, could be adapted for KS2

Aims

- To support word knowledge.
- To develop phonological awareness.
- To improve spelling.

Resources

- Large whiteboard or flipchart
- Mini-whiteboards or paper and pens

What to do

Phonic Clouds

1. Write a consonant cluster or long vowel phoneme on the board/ flipchart, for example, fl, tr, ea, oa and draw a cloud around it.

phonic cloud

bean team eat
sea leaf clean
please

2. In pairs, the children draw a cloud on their whiteboards and see how many words they can write that contain that phoneme. It is best to set a time limit, for example, two minutes.

3. The pair that writes the most words chooses the next phoneme for the class.

Word Sausages

1. This activity can be used to reinforce phonemes (for example, long vowel sounds) or other aspects of spelling, (for example, prefixes/suffixes).

2. Draw a sausage shape on the board and write a phoneme inside it, for example 'oo'. The children then work in pairs to see if they can make a 'string of sausages' which contains words with the 'oo' sound. Encourage the children to think of different ways of spelling the same sound. For example, for the 'oo' sausage string you could have *boot*, *new*, *blue*, *huge*.

Variation

● For KS2 you could have prefix clouds or root word clouds.

prefix cloud

un...
unhappy   unusual
unsafe   unknown
unable   unfasten

Spell that Word!

English spelling is tricky. This is because we use 44 sounds but only 26 letters. Spelling incorporates four dimensions: visual (how does a word *look*); phonological (how does a word *sound*); semantic (what does the word *mean* in context); and kinaesthetic (how does the word *feel* as its written). Playing word games is an enjoyable way to reinforce spelling strategies and build confidence.

Suitable for

KS1, KS2

Aim

- To develop strategies for spelling to include visual, phonological, semantic and kinaesthetic approaches.

Resources

- Paper and pencils
- Squared paper
- Dictionaries (optional)

What to do

Words within a Word

1. This activity can be played during spare moments in the day, such as registration.
2. Select a long word – 'communicate', for example. For younger children, use simpler words, e.g. window, kitchen, snowing.
3. Ask the children how many words they can make from the word.
4. A competitive edge can be added – which table can find the most words in a set period of time?

Hangman and Shannon's Game

Hangman

1. This well-known game still engages children. Shannon's Game is a slight variation. The aim is to guess the word from the blanks.

2. Select a word and represent it on a whiteboard, using a short, spaced line for each letter. So, 'mystery' would be represented as _ _ _ _ _ _ _.

3. Ask the children to fill the blanks. When a letter is guessed correctly, it is written in the appropriate blank space. For each incorrect guess, draw an element of the 'hangman'. The aim is to complete all the blanks before the hangman picture is finished.

Shannon's Game

1. Follow the first two steps for Hangman, above, but in this game the children have to guess the letters *in the order they appear* in the word. The children are praised for reasonable guesses even if they are incorrect. The aim is to encourage the children to think of possible sequences of letters.

Stairs

1. In pairs, the children take it in turns to complete a stairway, as shown below.

2. This could be played using a theme.

great
   r
   a
  plant
     e
     a
     c
    home
       n
       t
       e
       r

Square and Circle Words

1. Play this in pairs, using squared paper, if possible.
2. The aim is to complete a square or circle using letters.
3. Start with one word – the example given below began with 'table' and finished with 'teach'. Add other words with the same number of letters going down, across and up so the beginning and end of each word forms a corner for a square word.
4. The last word is the most difficult to complete.

```
T A B L E
E       Q
A       U
C       A
H O T E L
```

Variation

Hangman and Shannon's Game

- A competitive or time factor can be added to each version of the game. For example, which table guesses their word in the shortest time?

Words, Words, Words!

If children are to become effective spellers, they need to experiment and have fun with words, i.e. become 'word watchers'.

Suitable for

KS1, KS2

Aims

- To develop an awareness of how words look.
- To develop spelling strategies.

Resources

- Spelling posters, spelling games, a range of dictionaries, thesauruses

What to do

Play with Words

1. Have the children make new words by adding or deleting letters, then use the words in sentences and make up word puzzles.

Look at Words

1. Look for letter patterns, the shapes of words, letter sequences and find the tricky parts of words.
2. Encourage the children to 'photograph' words so that they have a picture of the *whole* word.

Listen to Words

1. Listen to the sounds in words – listen for the syllables or think of rhyming words.

. . . .

CHAPTER 3 WRITING **289**

Collect Words

1. Ask the children to look for words with a particular focus, such as from a visual point of view, or look out for sound patterns, homophones, prefixes or suffixes.

Word Stars

1. Ask the children to see how many words they can make using the letters in the central circle.

2. They can only use the letters in the outer circle once in each word. From the group of letters in this example they could make *boat*, *coat*, *goal*, *coal*, *foal*.

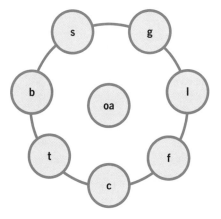

Word Sorts

1. There are two types of word sorts – closed and open.

2. In a *closed* sort, give the children the sorting criteria for a set of words. For example, ask them to pick out all the words with an 'ee' sound (spelled 'ee', 'ea' or 'ie') or all the words beginning with 'p'.

3. In an *open* sort, give the children a set of words, but leave it to them to decide how to sort them. The words could be from the tricky words list, topic words, words from their spelling journals and so on.

Additional materials to support this activity can be viewed/downloaded at
www.pearsoned.co.uk/glynne

More Ideas for Spelling

These are two practical activities that develop children's knowledge about spelling and help to improve their confidence.

Suitable for

KS1, KS2

Aims

- To develop spelling strategies.
- To support word knowledge.

Resources

- A variety of generic board games (for Board Game Spelling)

What to do

Board Game Spelling

1. Divide the children into groups and give each group a 'ready-made' board game, such as Snakes and Ladders or Bingo. (Each group needs a different board game.)

2. Ask the children to devise a new set of rules for that game which will incorporate their spelling words. For example, a group may decide that for Snakes and Ladders a player must first spell the word given to him or her, and if it is spelled correctly, they can then move their counter. An additional rule could be that they have to spell two words correctly before they can go up a ladder.

3. Once the groups have tried out their new versions they can write down the rules so that other groups can then play the games.

Word/Phrase of the Week

1. Choose a word or phrase that you'd like the children to use. Ask them to count how many times they can use that phrase or word throughout the week. Challenge them to use that word somewhere in their writing. This will help them to think about the meaning as well as how the word/s are written. The children could design a poster to illustrate the word or phrase.

2. Once the children are familiar with this activity they could be encouraged to take turns to share an unusual word with the class. They have to explain the meaning to the class and talk about why they selected the word. This activity helps to increase both children's interest and knowledge about words.

Hunt the Homophone

Homophones can be tricky for children as they sound the same but have different spellings. This activity helps them to investigate examples of homophones and learn about their meanings.

Suitable for

Upper KS1, KS2

Aims

- To support word knowledge.
- To improve spelling.

Resources

- Selection of homophones on cards (see example at **www.pearsoned.co.uk/ glynne**)
- Dictionaries (optional)
- Mini-whiteboards and pens

What to do

1. Divide the homophones into two sets so there is one example in each set. Display one set around the room and then give pairs of children two or three words each. They have to hunt for the homophone that matches each of their words. When they have finished they have to look at them and make sure they can explain the difference between the two words. Using mini-whiteboards they could put each of the words into a sentence or explain the meaning. How would they remember which word to use?

night knight

heard herd

2. Next each pair could work with another pair. They take turns at explaining their words without actually saying the words themselves. For example, for *night/knight* they could say '*One word means the opposite of day, the other is a soldier that wears armour.*' To increase the challenge the children could provide a clue for one of the words. The other pair then has to try and guess both words.

Variation

- Once the children are familiar with this activity you could get them to research their own homophones. Give them dictionaries so they can also find out the meanings of the words.

Spelling Challenges

This variety of activities supports children's spelling knowledge.

Suitable for

KS2, some activities could be adapted for KS1

Aims

- To develop spelling strategies.
- To support word knowledge.

Resources

- Mini-whiteboards and pens or paper and pens
- Dictionaries (for some activities)
- Magazines (for Spelling Search)

What to do

Word Chain

1. This activity encourages children to recognise possible letter combinations. The aim is to create a word chain in which the last two letters of a word form the first two letters of the next. Give the children a starter word, for example, 'stone'. The children work in pairs to make their word chain. For example, sto**ne**, **ne**ed**le**, **le**ng**th**, **th**read, **ad**vent**ure**, **re**ach, **ch**ain, **in**vite, etc.

2. You could see which is the quickest pair to make a chain with seven words or give the children a time limit, for example, you could challenge them to make the longest word chain in five minutes.

3. Alternatively, the children could score points, for example, two points for each letter used. If they have to find a word in a dictionary they only score one point for each letter.

Spelling Story Challenge

Ask the children to write a story using words with a particular pattern or word string, for example, words with 'ie' or words ending in 'ing'. It is probably best to limit the number of sentences, for example no more than five sentences.

Spelling search

Give pairs of children a magazine and tell them the type of spellings you want them to search for, for example, words ending in 'ly' or words with prefixes. Give them a time limit or a minimum number of words to locate.

Variation

- Younger children could search one page of text looking for particular phonemes, for example, consonant clusters.

Not Another Spelling List!

It is well known that children's spelling does not improve by just being presented with lists of words to learn. The words need to be incorporated into practical activities to help reinforce spelling knowledge. The following activities provide a range of ways to support the learning of different words.

Suitable for

KS2

Aims

- To support word knowledge.
- To improve spelling.

Resources

- Mini-whiteboards and pens or paper and pens
- Dictionaries (for some activities)
- Blank grids (for Spelling Crosswords)

What to do

Spelling Pyramid

This can be a paired or individual activity. Ask the children to write their words in a list from the easiest to the most challenging. They then write the easiest word at the top of the whiteboard or paper. They write the next word twice underneath and the third word three times underneath and so on until they have built their pyramid. See example below:

come

said   said

once once once

could could could could

people people people people people

Dictionary Challenge

1. Challenge the children to find all their focus words in a dictionary. They could do this in pairs or on an individual basis.

2. Set a time limit or ask the children to write down the meaning of each word.

3. You could ask pairs of children to race each other. Who can find the meaning in the shortest time?

Spelling Crosswords

1. Challenge the children to produce a crossword puzzle using the words on their list. It is best if the children work in pairs but they could work on an individual basis.

2. Provide each child or pair with a blank grid and a dictionary (so they can write the clues).

3. Once the children have produced the crossword they could swap with another pair and answer each other's clues.

Genre Spelling

1. Give the children a particular genre, for example, an adventure story, and ask them to use five or more of their spellings to write a short paragraph.

2. Over time try to vary the types of genre to give children an opportunity to be more creative. Fiction and poetry work very well but encourage children to try out a wider range of text types, for example, a diary entry, a letter or an advert. Once the children are familiar with the activity they could choose their own genre.

3. Alternatively, you could give the children five topic words or choose five words from a section in a dictionary. The latter would increase the children's vocabulary as well as supporting their spelling skills.

What's that Word?

The collection of games here encourage children to play with language and expand their vocabulary. They will then feel more confident to be adventurous with their writing.

Suitable for

KS2

Aims

- To broaden vocabulary.
- To support spelling knowledge.

Resources

- Mini-whiteboards or paper and pens
- Range of dictionaries
- Large hourglass timer or similar

What to do

Compound Word Games

Give us a Clue

1. This can be a paired or individual activity.
2. Give the children mini-whiteboards or paper and pens and ask them to draw pictures linked to the two parts of a compound word, such as teapot, football, cupboard, teabag, wardrobe, bathroom, carpet, floodlight, breakfast, shoebox, staircase, windmill. So, for teapot, they could draw a packet of tea and a cooking pot, as tea + pot = teapot.

3. The children's pictures can be displayed or made into a class book.

Fireball Words

1. Working either as a whole class or in pairs, one child says a word and the other has to reply with a compound word containing that word. So, for example, for the starter word 'fish', the compound word could be 'starfish'. Some other possible starter words are room, cup, fire, fish, ball, space.

Beat the Timer

1. Give the children a time limit of say, 30 seconds or 1 minute.

2. Ask them, 'How many compound words can you write before the time runs out?' and then turn the hourglass over or set the timer going.

Dictionary Games

Tell Me

1. Give the children a word and ask them to say or write a definition of it using only a certain number of words. So, for example, you could ask them to define 'boy' in four words – 'a young male person', for instance – or in two – 'male child'. This encourages them to be more precise in their use of language and increases their vocabulary.

Can You Beat the Dictionary?

1. This activity could take place after the children have been investigating or collecting new words.

2. Give one child a dictionary and then ask the rest of the class to think of or write the most difficult word they know.

3. Some of the children then take turns to say or show their word and the class have to see if they can explain the meaning of the word.

4. The child with the dictionary then reads out the definition – see which child's definition was the closest!

Variation

- **Give us a Clue** for some of the more difficult compound words – the children could show their pictures and see if the others can guess what the words are.

Spot the Syllables

This activity reinforces children's knowledge about syllables and helps to support their spelling.

Suitable for

KS2

Aims

- To develop an awareness of how words look.
- To improve knowledge about syllables.

Resources

- Mini-whiteboards and pens

What to do

1. This is a paired activity to encourage children to look for syllable boundaries. Give the children a selection of words with two or more syllables (see examples on page 302). Can they split the words into their separate syllables? How do they know when they have found a syllable? (They can check that each syllable has a vowel/vowel sound.)

2. The children could search for further two- or three-syllable words and then give them to another pair. You could give the children a theme to help them, for example, animals, transport, vegetables, fruit.

Examples of words with two or more syllables

Everyday words	More complex words
penguin	demonstrate
animal	photography
elephant	encourage
window	tomorrow
carrot	vocabulary
tomato	stationary
banana	beautiful
lorry	collection
scooter	character
motorbike	subtraction
apple	fertiliser
chimney	pronunciation

What's My Root?

This activity helps children to look carefully at words and to think about the different components, for example, root words, prefixes and suffixes.

Suitable for

KS2

Aims

- To investigate roots, prefixes and suffixes.
- To improve spelling.

Resources

- Examples of words with prefixes and suffixes for What's My Root? (see **www.pearsoned.co.uk/glynne**)
- Lists of root words, prefixes and suffixes for Mix and Match (see **www.pearsoned.co.uk/glynne**)
- Highlighter pens

What to do

What's My Root?

1. Look at several examples with the children and talk about the roots of each of the words. Explain that the root is the basic word and that we can add bits on to the beginning and/or end to make new words. The key is to remember that the root word is also a word in its own right.

2. The children then work in pairs to locate the root words from a selection they have been given. They could use highlighter pens to mark the root of each of the words.

Mix and Match

1. Investigate a selection of prefixes, suffixes and root words with the children. How many words can they make?

   - Can they make any words using more than one suffix? For example: *hope + ful + ly*.
   - Do they have to make any changes to the root word when adding suffixes? Are there any patterns? For example, what is the pattern for root words that end in *y* such as *beauty*, *happy*, *fancy*, *mercy*, etc.

Variation

- **What's My Root?** Give the children a root word and ask them to see how many new words they can make. For example, from the root word *talk* you can make *talked, talker, talking*.

Where Does That Word Come From?

The complexities of English spelling can be demystified by looking at the origins of words. Was a word originally French or Latin or Greek? By spending some time investigating the origins of words and looking at them closely they become memorable and easier to spell. These activities encourage investigation.

Suitable for

KS2

Aims

- To improve spelling.
- To investigate word origins.
- To play with language.

Resources

- Dictionaries
- Etymological dictionary (focuses on origins of words)
- Access to the Internet
- Card

What to do

Roots

1. Give the children a root of a word and ask for suggestions as to what it means.

2. Ask them to find as many words containing the root as they can. For example, for '*anti*', meaning 'opposite', they may suggest antisocial, antiseptic, antifreeze, antibiotic, antidote, antithesis.

3. Create a class etymological dictionary, highlighting the roots, origins and meanings of words and giving examples. It could be set out in a table, as follows.

Root	Origin	Meaning	Examples
tele	Greek	distant	telephone
			television
			telegraph

Create New Words

1. Following investigative work, it can be enjoyable to create *new* words and let the other class members guess what they might mean.

2. Alternatively, prefixes, suffixes and root words could be cut up and put onto pieces of card that could be moved around to create new words. For example, '*hydrograd*' – a water step, from '*hydro*', meaning water, and '*grad*', meaning step, or '*minimorph*' – a small structure, from '*mini*', meaning small, and '*morph*', meaning structure.

Investigate Change

1. Consider some abbreviations and ask the children, 'What was the original word?' Examples include 'plane' for 'aeroplane', 'net' for 'Internet' and 'cycle' for 'bicycle'.

2. Investigate some acronyms and consider whether or not an acronym is helpful. Some examples are IOC, for the International Olympic Committee, MTV, for Music Television, and SATs, for Standard Assessment Tests!

3. Discuss 'text speak' – are the abbreviations helpful?

Investigate Specialist Subject Language

1. Investigate words relating to a range of subjects. For example, in science we have 'experiment' and 'apparatus' – draw attention to the way these words begin and their etymology.

Spelling Prompts

> We need to help children to become more confident in using spelling strategies. These spelling prompts can support this process.

Suitable for

KS2

Aims

- To develop spelling strategies.
- To integrate spelling into everyday classroom routines.

Resources

- Spelling prompts (see page 308)

What to do

1. Display the prompts given in the boxes on posters and/or have small versions available on the children's tables.
2. Model how to use them. Initially, you will find that the children need regular reminders to ensure that they refer to the prompts during writing tasks.

To help you with your spelling

Think of how the word is used in the sentence.	Check that the word looks right.
Think about the meaning.	Underline the part you're not sure of.
Think of the base word.	Write the word another way.
Say the word slowly.	Look the word up – in class lists, books or a dictionary.
Listen to the sounds.	See if you know another word that is similar.

What to do if you can't spell a word

Guess Put a line under the word or circle it and check the spelling later.
Write as much as you can of the word and fill in the details later – bec_s for because, for example.
Syllabify Tap out the syllables, saying them quietly, then write the word bit by bit, such as yes/ter/day.
Write the word several ways and choose the one that looks right – lern, learn, lurn, for instance.
Refer to class lists, books around the room.
Use a dictionary.

Fiction activities

Story Openings

Here are some different strategies that help children improve their story openings. Young children can find it difficult to vary the beginnings of their stories, often falling back on the classic 'Once upon a time ...'. Providing them with a variety of story starters helps give them a wider range of ideas on which to build their stories. With older children, they need to be shown how to be more adventurous with their story openings.

Suitable for

KS1, KS2

Aim

- To experiment with different story openings.

Resources

- For KS1, different story starters (see page 313) on strips of card or a poster
- Range of good-quality narrative texts
- Mini-whiteboards and pens

What to do

Story Starters (KS1)

1. Have a selection of the story starter cards in a container.
2. Ask the children to pick one and then write a story that follows on from it.
3. Alternatively, display a poster of some different story starters. The children can then use these if they cannot think of their own story opening.

Story starters for KS1

- In a forest far away ...
- Many years ago ...
- Far away and long ago ...
- There was once a ...
- It happened one day that ...
- It was a dark and stormy night ...
- At the edge of the village ...
- Far across the galaxy on another planet ...
- I woke up in a strange place and saw ...
- It was a very unusual day in ...
- In a deep, dark dungeon ...
- The clock struck midnight ...

Variation

- Give all children the *same* story starter, but give some groups of children different characters to include. At the end of the session, compare the stories and see what the similarities and differences are. This shows children that there are different possibilities even when stories have started in the same way.

What to do

How Should I Begin? (KS2)

1. Encourage older children to collect interesting openings that they find while they are reading.

2. They could then put them in their reading journals or the class could make a book of effective openings. The following books are good examples.

   - *The Sheep-Pig* by Dick King-Smith (setting)

   - *Carrie's War* by Nina Bawden (setting)

   - *Why the Whales Came* by Michael Morpurgo (plot)

   - *Goodnight Mister Tom* by Michelle Magorian (setting)

   - *The Iron Man* by Ted Hughes (setting).

Hook the Reader (KS2)

1. Talk with the children about how to hook the attention of readers and make them want to read on. Have a list of things to avoid, such as long, boring descriptions of the weather, daily routines (getting up, eating breakfast) and dialogue that does not move the story on. Here are some examples of openings that the children can work on.

   - *Atmospheric* This can be a subtle start to a story and it sets the scene for whatever conflict or crisis follows. For example, *'The room was cold and damp. He could only make out the silhouettes of objects as the window was covered with brown paper.'*

   - *Dialogue* Immediately, there is a character and action, the story is ready to go. It is important, though, that the dialogue does not go on for too long.

   - *In the middle of things* This is a useful way to bring readers right into the heart of the action. It creates excitement and tension from the beginning. For example, *'Suddenly the scream pierced the night. I leapt to my feet. All was silent ... and then it came again, only this time closer to us.'*

   - *Contradictions* This method introduces a conflict or contradiction in the opening line, such as, *'Sometimes I adored Henry, but at other times I hated him.'*

   - *Questions* A lot of information can be given quickly and it draws the reader in. For example, *'Why was Jack's hair such an odd colour?'*

2. Model or discuss the different techniques and then ask the children to work in pairs to experiment with the various openings.

3. You will need to work on this over several sessions so that the children become familiar with using the different strategies.

Further sources of information

- Some of the ideas for KS2 have been adapted from *Improving Writing at KS2* by Surrey LEA and 'New Beginnings', an article by Alan Peat in *Literacy and Learning* (December 1999/January 2000).

In the End

Children can often run out of ideas towards the end of a story and then think only of clichéd endings – 'It was all a dream' or 'Then we went home and had our tea'! The strategies given here can help children to be more creative with their endings and take more risks in their writing.

Suitable for

KS2

Aims

- To look at elements of story structure.
- To encourage children to use a wider range of story endings.

Resources

- Poster displaying different story endings
- Range of good-quality narrative texts
- Mini-whiteboards and pens

What to do

Hunt the Ending

1. Encourage the children to be 'story detectives', their job being to hunt for effective endings in the different texts.

2. The results of their searches can then be displayed on a poster in the classroom. Here are some examples of story endings that the children might find:

   - it had finished, at last
   - the horror was over and we were all safe

- there was home at last – they had made it
- and even to this day ...
- he never ever went back
- so that was the end of the King.

How Does it End?

1. Start by talking with the children about different types of endings and the effects they have.

2. Ask the children to try them out, working in pairs and using mini-whiteboards. Here are some ideas for types of endings they could experiment with.

   - The ending mirrors the beginning, for example, use the same words, but change the mood or situation.

   - Endings with a twist. The twist should come very close to the end – preferably in the last paragraph – and be described in only a few words.

   - The narrator reflects on what has happened. For example, '*Sarah knew she should have listened to her grandma.*'

   - One of the characters has the last word, such as '*I promise, Mum,*' George whispered, '*I won't do it again.*'

   - The main character thinks or reflects on what has happened.

'What If ...?' Game

1. Playing this game prompts the children to think about different possible endings to a story.

2. Ask the children to consider the following kinds of questions.

   - What if he could get back/couldn't get back?

   - What if she stayed as small as a mouse?/What if she returned to normal size?

   - What if they became friends after all?/What if they never spoke again?

Story Ideas

These are different strategies for helping children develop their story ideas, particularly for interesting settings.

Suitable for

KS1, KS2

Aims

- To develop the imagination.
- To develop aspects within a story, such as settings.

Resources

- Story boxes – shoeboxes or other small boxes with a range of small artefacts, such as 'small world' toys, unusual buttons, shells, keys, old coins, bits of string and ribbon
- Paper and pencils

.What to do

Think of a Setting (KS1, KS2)

1. This is a type of 'imagination' exercise that can be done before the children start to work on stories.

2. Ask them to sit in a circle, then close their eyes and imagine that they are in a particular setting of their own choosing.

3. When their eyes are open again, ask them to describe the setting and where they are. Here are some examples of the kinds of responses children could give.

   - I am sitting outside a cave waiting for the dragon to come out.
   - I am in a forest and it is dark and spooky.
   - I am hiding in a cupboard and eating a piece of cake.

- I am on a horse flying through the air.
- I am stepping through a wardrobe into a magical land.

Change the Setting (KS2)

1. Talk with the children about how to use the setting to create atmosphere. You could model an example by taking an ordinary place (such as a library, school, shop) and making it seem scary.

2. Involve the children by asking, 'What is hidden, what looks unusual, what is out of place?'

3. Show the children how certain aspects can change the atmosphere of a place, such as time of day, the weather, season and so on.

4. Then the children can work in pairs. Give them a setting and ask them to change it in some way.

5. You could give some children different challenges, such as to change just one aspect or change two out of three aspects. Talk with them about how the atmosphere would change – what difference would it make to the story? Here is an example of this process.

   - *Original setting* A beach on a sunny afternoon in summer.
   - *Change one aspect* (weather) A beach on a *rainy afternoon* in summer.
   - *Change two out of three aspects* (weather and season) A beach on a *windy afternoon* in *winter*.

Story Boxes (KS1, KS2)

1. These extremely versatile resources can be used in a variety of ways. Here are some ideas.

   - Young children can work in pairs or small groups to make a story box linked to a well-known story. They could use 'small world' toys and drawings for the characters and setting.
   - The children can use their story boxes to help them retell a story and then produce a written version.
   - Alternatively, the children might create their own story by first building a story box. This process helps them to experiment and develop their ideas before putting them down on paper.

- A whole-class or group activity for older children is to show them a story box containing a wide range of artefacts – a key, piece of lace, old coin and button, for example. Then, ask them to think about the objects, for example, where they would find these things. Who might own them? The children can discuss their ideas and devise a story that links the objects together in some way.

- Have groups of children gather together some objects (or draw them). Once they have produced their story boxes they can swap them with another group. Ask the groups to look at the objects and create a story that includes them. This can be linked to a drama activity so that the children can explore their story orally before writing it.

What Happens Next?

Two different strategies are included here to help children improve the structure of their stories. Young children need a great deal of support with story structure and the first strategy ensures that there is a beginning, middle and end to their stories. A number of older children write wonderful beginnings to stories, then lose the plot halfway through. The stories then tend to end too quickly or fade away rather weakly. The second technique supports children in developing ideas for the middle of their stories in order to improve their structure.

Suitable for

KS1, KS2

Aim

- To look at story structure.

Resources

- Paper and pens
- Story Consequences prompts (see page 321)

What to do

Story Consequences or Pass on the Story (KS1)

1. Play the game like traditional Consequences or leave the paper unfolded so that each child can see what has gone on before.

2. The children can work in pairs or small groups.

3. Either write the prompts on a flipchart/interactive whiteboard or give copies to the children in the form of a writing frame. See the example given below.

    1. One day ....

       (Introduce two characters – one male, one female.)

    2. They were ....

    3. Suddenly ....

    4. Next ....

    5. At last ....

Stuck in the Middle (KS2)

1. Sit the children in groups of four or five and tell them the beginning of a story.

2. Then, give each child in each group one minute to write the next part of the story.

3. When the time is up, they pass their writing to the child on their right and he or she continues the story. This time they have one and a half minutes to write the next part.

4. Repeat this two or three more times, but make sure that you give the children a little longer to write (say, two minutes) as they need a little longer each time to read what has been written already.

5. In this way, the children are encouraged to continue the story by considering past actions and so avoid long sections of dialogue with no action or description. It is important to emphasise to them that they should not end the story – they must stay in the middle!

Story Shapes

Children need to hear and read a wide range of stories. Examining the way a story is put together helps children to plan their own stories. These interactive activities look at two different story structures.

Suitable for

KS1, KS2

Aims

- To look at story structure.
- To create simple story plans.

Resources

- A large space, if possible
- Long strips of paper
- A3 paper, if possible
- Card

What to do

The Quest

1. Many traditional tales are linear. Often the youngest son is sent to seek his fortune and he encounters adventures on his way to a successful conclusion. This can be represented diagrammatically.

| The youngest son | sets off | crosses a river | climbs a mountain | cuts down a forest | rescues and marries a princess |

2. It helps to physically walk through a story. So do this activity in a large space, if possible, modelling it first.

3. Using the long strips of paper, ask the children, in groups of two or three, to plan a story, writing what happens at each stage of the story at the appropriate place on the line.

4. Walk through the events in the story, literally. One child can narrate.

5. The events can then be noted down and used as a basic plan for writing.

Story Arch

1. Many stories are divided into five sections, which can be represented by a story arch. The classic story of Cinderella follows this pattern.

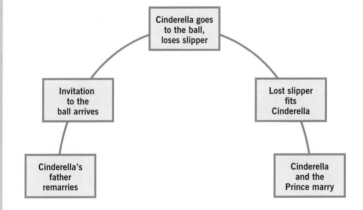

2. Use the tale of Cinderella to illustrate how the five sections of a story work.

   - *Beginning* Cinderella's father remarries and the stepmother and her daughters treat Cinderella badly.
   - *Lead up* The invitation to the ball arrives.
   - *High point* Cinderella goes to the ball and loses her glass slipper.
   - *Lead down* The Prince tries to find the owner of the lost glass slipper.
   - *Ending* Cinderella and the Prince marry.

3. Next, in pairs, ask the children to recreate another traditional tale using a story arch to record the key events – Little Red Riding Hood or The Three Little Pigs work well. Use A3 paper for the sections of the arch, if possible.

4. When they are familiar with this basic five-part structure, the children can plan their own stories. It is a good idea to model this, taking ideas from the class, before asking the children to work in pairs or individually.

Variation

- For the Quest, when working with younger children, cut the paper into the shape of stepping stones. They can then write each section of the story on a 'stone' and step from one part of the story to the next.

Additional materials to support this activity can be viewed/downloaded at **www.pearsoned.co.uk/glynne**

Circles and Graphs

These activities introduce some more story shapes and make an explicit link between reading and writing. They add a visual dimension to story planning.

Suitable for

KS1, KS2

Aims

- To make explicit links between reading and writing.
- To apply a range of story plans.

Resources

- Graphs
- Set of cards of unusual events
- A selection of stories with a circular structure
- A range of artefacts

What to do

Story Graphs

1. With younger children, start with a discussion of an ordinary day when something unusual happens.
2. Use the graph to show how this could be represented.
3. Model an unusual day, creating a similar graph (see page 326).
4. Give the children a graph and ask them to work in pairs to create the story of the graph.
5. Have the set of cards ready to suggest something unusual that might happen, you might find a golden ring, you might receive an invitation to a special event or you might get a mystery phone call.

6. The children then retell their stories orally and later transfer the structure to create their own story plans.

Example of a Story Graph for KS1

An unusual day

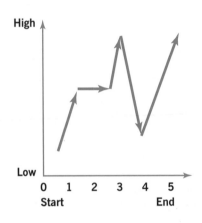

- You get up in the morning.
- You get your picnic ready.
- You enjoy your picnic and find a purse containing £10,000, which you give to the police.
- You go home (which is dull after all the excitement).
- You are given a reward.

What to do

The Interloper

1. Ask the children what happens when someone or something upsets the status quo. In Philippa Pearce's *The Battle of Bubble and Squeak* (E.P. Dutton, 1979) the family's relationships are challenged when some gerbils arrive! The interloper is represented by this diagram – the circle

being the status quo (the family living their day-to-day lives) and the line representing the interloper (the gerbils, upsetting the family's equilibrium).

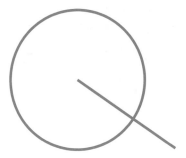

2. The children can then develop their own stories that rely on an interloper to precipitate change. Here are some suggestions for starting points for interloper stories:

- a long-lost relative suddenly appears and needs somewhere to stay
- your parents have to move to a new town
- new people move in next door and they have some strange habits
- a new child arrives at your school and makes friends with your best friend
- a motorway is to be built and it means that the local adventure playground will be demolished.

Circular Stories

1. Some stories have a circular structure – that is, the end brings us back to the beginning. Many of Anthony Browne's tales have this structure, such as *Willy the Wimp* and *Piggybook*.
2. Read some circular stories to the children.
3. Sit in a circle to retell the tales.
4. Use artefacts as prompts to create a class circular story.
5. In small groups, get the children to create more stories that can be put into a class big book.

Variations

- Block graphs can be used to represent cumulative tales, such as The Gingerbread Boy and The Enormous Turnip.
- Make up class cumulative stories. Perhaps one could be based on everyone who works in the school, such as the following.

> The headteacher arrived at school one day and couldn't find his/her keys so he/she went to find the caretaker.

> The caretaker looked for the keys but couldn't find them, so she/he went to look for the cook.

> The cook looked for the keys but couldn't find them so he/she went to look for the secretary.

Story Planners and Prompts (KS1)

It is important to provide support for children when they are planning stories as many of them find it a difficult process.

Suitable for

KS1

Aims

- To create simple story plans.
- To think about story structure.

Resources

- Range of story plans and prompts

What to do

Storyboard

1. This planning format is mainly suitable for younger children, but it can be used with older struggling writers.
2. Ask the children to draw simple pictures in the boxes, then make brief notes underneath to answer the questions (see example on page 330). It is important to model the process of writing the notes otherwise some children may start to write the whole story on the sheet.

Simple Story Planner

1. As with the storyboard, you will need to model how to use this story planner.

Storyboard

1	2	3	4
....	....	....	....
....	....	....	....
....	....	....	....
....	....	....	....
....	....	....	....
....	....	....	....
Who is in the story?	Where does it take place?	What is the main thing that happens?	What happens in the end?

Story planner

Where does the story happen? ....
....

Who is in it? ....
....

What do they do? ....
....

What happens at the end? ....
....

Story Prompts

1. Below is a selection of prompts to link with different aspects of the story. It is not intended that you use all of them – select the most appropriate ones for your children. They can be put on to a planning frame or used as oral prompts in guided writing sessions.

- Setting
  - Where is your story set?
  - What time of day is it?
  - What is the weather like?
- Characters
  - Who is the main character?
  - Who else is in the story?
- Opening
  - How will your story start?
  - Introduce your main character.
  - How is he or she feeling?
- Problem
  - What is your character's problem?
- Main event
  - What happens to the main character?
- Ending
  - What happens at the end?
  - How is the main character feeling?

Additional materials to support this activity can be viewed/downloaded at
www.pearsoned.co.uk/glynne

Story Planners and Prompts (KS2)

In Key Stage 2, children need to be more adventurous with their story plots. The story planners and prompts given here can help to scaffold the children's ideas.

Suitable for

KS2

Aims

- To apply a range of story plans.
- To think about the structure of stories.

Resources

- Range of story plans and prompts (see pages 333–4)
- Mini-whiteboards and pens

What to do

Story Planner

1. Use the 'Fiction Button' on this planner as a useful way to get children to think about the movement of a story's plot. Talk with them about this imaginary button and ask them what would happen if it was pressed. Would something happen to the main character? Would there be an interloper? (See Circles and Graphs, page 326).

Story Pyramid

1. This useful technique encourages the children to think about the essence of their stories.

2. Initially, model how to use the pyramid (see page 333) by linking it to a story that you have read with the children.

3. Work on the first four steps together, then get the children to work in pairs on mini-whiteboards to complete the last four steps.

Story Planner

Setting: Who and where?

Fiction button: How does the story get going?

Problems and solutions

In the end: The characters' views and feelings.

Story Pyramid

1. ......

2. ....

3. ....

4. ....

5. ....

6. ....

7. ....

8. ....

1. Write the name of the main character.
2. Write two words describing the main character.
3. Write three words describing the setting.
4. Write four words stating the problem in the story.
5. Write five words describing the first event.
6. Write six words describing the second event.
7. Write seven words describing the third event.
8. Write eight words describing the solution to the problem.

Story Prompts

1. Here is a selection of prompts to help the children consider the different elements within a story. Select some to put onto a planning frame or use them as oral prompts in guided writing sessions.

- *Setting*
  - Think about the place, time of day and the weather.
- *Characters*
  - Have no more than three main characters.
  - Think of interesting names.
  - Use a few special details.
  - Decide how your character(s) feel.
- *Opening*
  - Think of an interesting way to start your story.
  - Grab the reader's attention.
  - Set the scene.
  - Introduce at least one main character.
- *Problem*
  - What gets the story going?
  - What happens to the main characters?
  - What is the main event?
- *Resolution*
  - How are the problems sorted out?
- *Ending*
  - What happens at the end?
  - How are the main characters feeling?
  - What have they learned?

Additional materials to support this activity can be viewed/downloaded at
www.pearsoned.co.uk/glynne

What Happened When ...?

Using fairy tales and nursery rhymes

This activity builds on children's knowledge of fairy tales and nursery rhymes. It can be a self-sustaining oral activity or an enjoyable introduction to shared, paired or individual written work.

Suitable for

KS1

Aims

- To develop imagination.
- To create an explicit link between reading and writing.
- To use knowledge of traditional rhymes and tales as a starting point for writing.

Resources

- Three sets of cards: one red set for characters, one blue set for places, one yellow set for times (available at **www.pearsoned.co.uk/glynne**)
- Copies of table (see page 336)
- A collection of fairy tales and nursery rhymes

What to do

1. Play this game with the whole class or in small groups. The aim is to try and answer the question 'What happened when ... ?'

2. Put the cards out in four piles if using all of them (two piles for characters). The times and places cards are optional but suggest an extra dimension.

3. Ask the children to each turn over one card from each pile and place them in the order of the headings in the table (see page 336) to answer

the question 'What happened when ... ?' Some unusual pairings will be created! For example, What happened when the Owl and the Pussycat met the Gingerbread Boy in a restaurant at midnight?

4. Discuss the feasibility of the sentences that have been created.

5. In groups, ask the children to use their sentences to create a story in which the characters are featured. These could be improvised and the stories could be brought up to date. A class book of unusual fairy tales could be produced.

What happened when?

Character (red cards)	met	character (red cards)	in|at on|by	place (blue cards)	when (yellow)
Cinderella	met	Goldilocks	at	the shop	at midday
Humpty Dumpty	met	The wolf	on	a farm	at night
Jack	met	Old Macdonald	by	a river	last week

Additional materials to support this activity can be viewed/downloaded at www.pearsoned.co.uk/glynne

Copycat

Descriptions of character and setting

> This activity explicitly invites innovation – using someone else's work! Taking an extract from a well-known story, the children are encouraged to consider how an effective text has been assembled and use its structure as a model for their own writing. This is a quick paired activity and produces instant, effective outcomes, especially for descriptive writing relating to characters and settings.

Suitable for

KS2

Aims

- To make explicit links between reading and writing.
- To develop character and setting.

Resources

- Texts that contain descriptions of characters and settings
- Create a cloze passage from the selected text – deleting specific words and phrases (see page 338)

What to do

1. Select a short description of a character or setting from a well-known and well-written story (Roald Dahl's work is full of detailed character descriptions that work well for this activity).
2. Divide the children into pairs, then give each pair a copy of the extract. You may wish to model the procedure first.
3. Read the extract together, pointing out any effective phrases or unusual words.

4. Present the children with copies of the cloze extract you have prepared.

5. Ask the children to come up with their own version of the descriptive piece and fill in the blanks with different words and phrases relating to their version. In this way, they will create a different character and/ or setting. It is not necessary to fill in the blanks so that they exactly match the original – adaptations can be made – but this activity provides a starting point for writing and an opportunity to create a character or setting quite quickly. It gives instant structure and form to the new piece of writing, which helps to develop children's confidence.

Worked example

This example shows how the the whole process works. The passage used is from *Uncle Ernest* by Allan Sillitoe (in M. Kilduff, R. Hamer and J. McCannon, *Working with Short Stories*, Cambridge University Press, 1991).

Original passage

Uncle Ernest

A middle-aged man wearing a dirty raincoat, who badly needed a shave and looked as though he hadn't washed for a month, came out of a public lavatory with a cloth bag of tools folded beneath his arm. Standing for a moment on the edge of the pavement to adjust his cap – the cleanest thing about him – he looked casually to left and right and when the flow of traffic had eased off, crossed the road ... Ernest Brown was the upholsterer.

Cloze passage

A _____ wearing a _____, who looked as though _____, came out of the _____ with a _____ beneath his arm. Standing for a moment on the edge of the pavement to _____ he looked _____ to the left and right and, when the flow of traffic had eased off, crossed the road. ... _____ the _____.

This could become

Jake

A *youngish man* wearing a *battered leather jacket,* who looked as though *he was afraid of no one*, came out of the *garage* with a *large metal box* beneath his arm. Standing for a moment on the edge of the pavement to *make sure he wasn't being followed – as was his habit* – he looked *suspiciously* to the left and right and, when the flow of traffic had eased off, crossed the road. ... *Jake Turnbull was* the *local gang leader.*

Draw a Character

This activity is very useful for helping to develop characters for narrative work, a composite character being created using mini-whiteboards. Children of all abilities can participate fully and the outcome may lead to written or drama work.

Suitable for

KS1, KS2

Aim

- To develop characters for narrative.

Resources

- Mini-whiteboards and pens

What to do

1. This is a very structured activity that aims to gradually and collectively build up a character. It works most successfully if the children are sitting at tables in groups of about six. If possible, model the activity first with a teaching assistant, particularly when working with younger children.

2. Ask the children to draw the outline of a face on their mini-whiteboards. Emphasise that the face should fill the whiteboard. Ask them to pass their whiteboard, clockwise, to the next person at their table.

3. Then ask them to draw in the eyes of the character before passing the whiteboards on clockwise again.

4. Next, ask them to add a nose and pass the whiteboard on once more.

5. Next, the children add a mouth before passing on the whiteboards.

6. Next, the children add the ears (perhaps with earrings) before passing on the whiteboards.

7. They then draw in the hair and pass on the whiteboards.

8. Finally, they name the characters – both a first and a last name, as well as a title if they wish. This can lead to some interesting names – Lady Samantha Carrington-Jones or Master Sandeep Patel, for example. If the children find it difficult to come up with names it's helpful to have a standby list – it can also be used in drama sessions. The 'list' can take the form of three piles of cards in different colours, with titles written on red cards, first names on blue cards and family names or surnames on yellow cards, for example. The children simply pick one card from each pile to devise their character's names.

Additional materials to support this activity can be viewed/downloaded at **www.pearsoned.co.uk/glynne**

Make a Story

This strategy helps children to think about elements within a story and provides them with some starting points.

Suitable for

KS1

Aims

- To provide starting points for stories.
- To look at story elements (character, setting, problem).
- To develop children's imagination.

Resources

- Three sets of cards (characters on red, settings on yellow, problems on blue)

What to do

1. It is a good idea to model this activity so that the children understand how to use the cards.

2. In pairs or groups, the children put the three sets of cards face down. They take a card from each pile and then use them to begin to compose a story. They could tell the story orally first to help them organise their ideas.

3. Here are some suggestions for words that could be written on each set of cards.

   - For *characters*, boy, girl, cat, dog, man, woman (these are deliberately bland so that the children can add their own descriptive details).

   - For *settings*, in the park, at the shops, in a village, at the farm, in the woods, at the zoo.

- For *problems*, got stuck in a tree, lost some money, fell down a hole, fell into a river, got lost, met a dangerous animal.

4. Initially, the children tend to link the three elements in just one or two sentences, so encourage them to add in more details by getting the other children to ask them questions using Why?, What?, Where?, When?, Who?. For example, if a pair of children pick *'girl'*, *'at the farm'* and *'fell down a hole'*, they can expand on an initial linking of these elements by saying *what* she looked like, *why* she was at the farm, *where* the hole was and *what* happened next.

Variation

- Instead of using sets of cards, you could use three large blank dice – one for characters, one for settings and the other for problems. The pairs of children could throw each die in turn to prompt the three elements for their story.

Additional materials to support this activity can be viewed/downloaded at **www.pearsoned.co.uk/glynne**

Set the Scene

Children can find it hard to describe the settings in their stories. These strategies can help them to provide more details and make their writing more interesting.

Suitable for

KS2, could be adapted for KS1

Aims

- To create interesting settings.
- To think about the different aspects of a setting.
- To investigate the use of descriptive language.

Resources

For Guess the Setting

- Settings cards (see below)
- A3 (or larger) sheets of paper and pens

For Sense It!

- Pictures of different settings, such as postcards, pictures from magazines
- Sense charts (see page 346)

What to do

Guess the Setting

1. The children need to be in small groups for this activity.

2. One child from each group picks a settings card and then returns to his or her group. It is important that the groups do not see each other's cards. Some examples of settings you could use are: *under the sea, in a castle, on a spaceship, on an island, in a rainforest, in a desert, inside a cave, on a mountain.*

3. The children in each group place their settings card in the middle of their large sheet of paper and discuss the setting quietly. They think of things (nouns) associated with the setting and write these on the paper.

4. Next, they give more information about each noun by adding words that describe it, for example, for the setting 'Under the sea', *beautiful* mermaid, *rusty* shipwreck, *brittle* coral, *wriggling* octopus, *scary* shark, *floating* anemone, *graceful* manta ray, *tiny* seahorse, *gigantic* crab, *spiky* starfish.

5. When the groups have finished, display their sheets of paper (without the settings cards). The groups can then try to guess each other's settings using the nouns and adjectives as clues.

Sense It!

1. This technique can be used by the children when they are creating settings for their own stories. By adding sensory details they can bring their settings alive. You will need to emphasise to them, however, that too *much* description can slow down the pace of the narrative.

2. It is a good idea to start this activity by modelling it to the whole class. Show the children a picture of a setting, making sure that it is large enough for them to see, for example, you could use the interactive whiteboard for this instead.

3. With the children, in pairs, ask them to think about their different senses. What would they see, hear, smell, touch or taste in the setting? This could be done orally or they could make notes on a mini-whiteboard. Model how to begin to write a description of the setting using some of the children's ideas.

4. Each pair could then have a postcard or picture and use the sense prompts to think about the setting. They could use a sense chart (see page 346) to make notes, then use these to write a short description of their setting.

Sense chart

Put notes about each sense in the right column.				
Setting:...				
Sight	Sound	Smell	Touch	Taste

Variations

- **Guess the Setting** For younger children, it is probably best to do this activity with the whole class. Choose one of the settings and begin to model how to add words associated with it. You will not be able to play the game as set out above, but instead, ask the children to work with a partner to think of descriptive words that *link* with the setting.
- **Sense It!** This idea could be used with younger children, but it would have to be modelled very carefully first. For the best results, have the children focus on just a couple of senses, asking, for example, 'What do you see or hear?'

Additional materials to support this activity can be viewed/downloaded at
www.pearsoned.co.uk/glynne

Playing to the Audience

Children have practical experience of role play from the early years. Putting improvisations into a structured form helps them to understand how narrative can be developed through dialogue and action.

Suitable for

KS2

Aims

- To understand the playscript format.
- To change from a narrative to a playscript form.
- To make meaningful links between oral and written activities.

Resources

- A selection of plays and corresponding novels, if possible

What to do

1. Share the selected playscripts and, if possible, their corresponding novels.
2. Point out the conventions of writing a playscript:
   - lack of speech marks
   - instructions
   - how a scene is set
   - layout.
3. Take a short extract from one of the novels.
4. Model how this can be rewritten as a playscript.
5. In groups, the children take other extracts and create playscripts from one extract.

6. Point out how the dialogue and actions tell the story. Here is an example of an extract and, following it, a parallel playscript.

> Kate couldn't sleep, she was too excited. Tomorrow she would be leaving for a long-awaited trip to America. She lay in bed for what seemed hours trying to rest but it was impossible. Eventually she decided to call her friend, Jo. She reached for her mobile, which she kept by the side of her bed in a special holder shaped like Winnie the Pooh, and dialled. No answer – it went straight to voicemail. How infuriating!
>
> As her head hit the pillow, Kate's mobile rang.
>
> 'Hi,' she stammered, picking it up and noticing Jo's number illuminated on the screen, 'you took your time.'
>
> 'Oh I've got plenty of time but your friend does not,' came the muffled reply of a voice that clearly did not belong to Jo!
>
> **Scene** – *bedroom at night, containing a bed and bedside table. Girl lying in bed.*
>
> **Kate** – *lies in bed, moving around restlessly.*
>
>> If only I could get a bit of sleep. I've got to be up early. I can't wait for tomorrow – America, here I come!
>
> *Picks up the mobile phone from holder on bedside table, dials and waits – there is clearly no reply.*
>
>> Oh, typical! No one's ever around when you need them.
>
> *Kate lies down in bed again and prepares to sleep. Phone rings. Kate picks it up.*
>
>> Hi – about time, too – you certainly took your time!
>
> *Kate pauses and listens to the reply.*
>
>> What did you say? Who are you and what are you doing with Jo's phone?

7. In groups, ask the children to devise simple improvisations. It's a good idea to give them a theme, such as a mystery gift arrives, a telephone call gives unexpected news, an invitation has to be turned down and so on.

8. The children then create simple playscripts based on their short improvisations.

Poetry activities

Alliterative Alphabet

This is an enjoyable way to practise initial sounds. The activity focuses on alliteration, which is the repetition of sounds in poems or rhymes, usually at the beginning of words.

Suitable for

KS1

Aims

- To practise listening to and writing initial sounds.
- To create alliterative sentences.

Resources

- A collection of alphabet poems and tongue-twisters

What to do

1. Read a selection of the alphabet poems.

2. Share the tongue-twisters.

3. As a class or with a group, create an alliterative alphabet with the children – an animal theme often works well. This can then be illustrated and made into a book or used as a display.

4. A poem using the alphabet can be built up in stages, starting with nouns, adding the adjectives (alliteration) and possibly developing the sentences further.

5. The outcome can be a whimsical nonsense poem, such as the one on page 353, showing three stages.

- *First stage*
  - 'A' is for an *ant*.
  - 'B' is for a *bat*.
  - 'C' is for a *cat*.
  - 'D' is for a *dinosaur*.
  - 'E' is for an *elephant*.
- *Second stage, adding some alliteration*
  - 'A' is for an *angry* ant.
  - 'B' is for a *barmy* bat.
  - 'C' is for a *careless* cat.
  - 'D' is for a *daft* dinosaur.
  - 'E' is for an *elegant* elephant.
- *Third stage, further development*
  - 'A' is for an angry ant *who was anxious*.
  - 'B' is for a barmy bat *who was brainy*.
  - 'C' is for a careless cat *who was creative*.
  - 'D' is for a daft dinosaur *who was daring*.
  - 'E' is for an elegant elephant *who was excellent*.

Variation

- Use numbers one to ten to create number rhymes, such as the following.

  One is fun.

  Two are my shoes.

  Three are those trees.

Rhyme Time

This activity helps children to experiment with rhyming words. By using the structure of a nursery rhyme they only need to focus on one small element.

Suitable for

- Early years, KS1

Aims

- To explore and work with rhyming patterns.
- To develop phonological awareness.

Resources

- A variety of nursery rhymes
- Whiteboard or flipchart

What to do

1. Start by reading a well-known nursery rhyme with the children, such as 'Hickory Dickory Dock'. Identify the rhyming words with the children and highlight them.

2. Ask the children to talk with their partners to see if they can think of any words that rhyme with 'dock'. Make a collection of the children's suggestions on a whiteboard or flipchart.

3. Write alternative verses with the children using some of the rhyming words they contributed. For example:

   Hickory dickory dock

   The mouse ran up the sock

Hickory dickory dock

The mouse ran up the rock

4. Ask the children to complete one or two additional verses and illustrate them. Some of them could work with a different rhyming pattern, such as Hickory Dickory Dare.

5. The children could make 'Hickory Dickory' books in the shape of a 'grandfather clock'.

Variations

An alternative example linked to 'Humpty Dumpty'.

- Start in a similar way as before, e.g. reading the rhyme and highlighting the rhyming words. Ask the children if they can think of any more words that rhyme with 'all'. Make a list and then write some additional verses.
- You could write some alternative versions using different rhyming patterns e.g. *hill, chair, mat, bed* and *tree*. See examples below:

  Humpty Dumpty sat on a mat
  Humpty Dumpty had a cat

  Humpty Dumpty sat on a chair
  Humpty Dumpty ate a pear

- The children could make 'Humpty Dumpty' books in the shape of an egg.

Lovely Lists

This activity introduces young children to writing simple poems using repetition and alliteration. The form offers them a ready-made structure and is ideal for shared work. Circle time presents a good opportunity for creating an instant collaborative poem using this method.

Suitable for

KS1

Aim

- To understand how language can be used for effect.

Resources

- List of starter sentences (can be made into a set of cards)
- Selection of alphabet poems and tongue-twisters

What to do

1. Ask the children to sit in a circle.
2. Using the starter sentences, the first child completes a chosen sentence orally.
3. A second child adds his or her line. Here is an example of the kinds of sentences produced from one starter sentence.
   - My favourite time of day is when I'm read a bedtime story.
   - My favourite time of day is when I get out of bed.
   - My favourite time of day is playtime.
   - My favourite time of day is lunchtime.

4. To build on this, ask the children to add more to the sentences by using 'because' at the end. The examples given on page 356 could then look like this.

- My favourite time of day is when I'm read a bedtime story because I love to listen.
- My favourite time of day is when I get out of bed because I'm ready for the day ahead.
- My favourite time of day is playtime because I can see all my friends.
- My favourite time of day is lunchtime because I'm always hungry.

5. You can be the scribe, noting all the contributions. These can be put into a book and illustrated. In this way, a range of class poetry books is gradually built up. Ensure they are accessible to the children as they love to identify their own sentences.

Guess Who?

This activity is an enjoyable way to apply metaphors. It is similar to the well-known game Twenty Questions.

Suitable for

KS2

Aim

- To develop the concept of metaphor.

Resources

- A list of categories, on the board or put onto card (see page 360)

What to do

1. A good way to begin this activity is by playing the traditional game of Twenty Questions, in which you have to find out someone or something's name by asking a maximum of 20 questions. You are only allowed to know the category, which could be animal, vegetable or mineral.

2. Introducing 'if' to the questions adds a metaphorical dimension.

3. Choose one child to sit in the middle of a circle.

4. Ask him or her to think of someone. It could be a child in the class, a well-known person or a celebrity – a politician, pop star, soap star or film star, for example. If the child chooses another child in the class, it's important to lay down ground rules – nothing unpleasant is allowed!

5. Show the children the list of categories written on the board or turn over a card.

6. The children then take turns to find the mystery character by using 'if' to begin each question. Here are some examples.

- If the person was a *car*, what car would he/she be?
- If the person was a *drink*, what type of drink would he/she be?
- If the person was a *building*, what type of building would he/she be?
- If the person was a *lesson*, which lesson would he/she be?
- If the person was an item of *furniture*, what would he/she be?

7. Be the children's scribe and write the answers on the board. For example, the answers to the questions above might be as follows, producing a simple list poem.

> *He's a racing car.*
> *He's fizzy cola.*
> *He's a tall skyscraper.*
> *He would be a PE lesson.*
> *He would be a leather sofa.*

8. Next, ask the children to guess who the person could be. This often produces a lively discussion.

9. To conclude the activity, the poem can be developed further, modelling how this is done initially. Essentially, this involves asking the children to be more specific, resulting in a poem such as the following.

> *He's a racing car, driving at 120 mph around the windswept track.*
> *He's a sparkling glass of fizzy cola, spilling onto the table top.*
> *He's a tall building, reaching for the sky.*
> *He's an energetic rugby lesson.*
> *He's a soft black leather sofa, awaiting the end of the day.*

Variations

- This can lead on to sharing and writing riddles.
- A book of the poems can be collated, entitled 'Guess Who?'

Categories

Transport
Building
Flowers
Trees
Food
Drink
Furniture
Book
Entertainment
Country
Lesson
Holiday

Playful Poems

Children enjoy the rhyme and rhythm as well as the brevity of poems. Read poems to the class in those cracks of time that occur on a daily basis. They will begin to appreciate the way poets play with language and how a few carefully chosen words make an impact. The acrostic and limerick forms featured in these activities make a good starting point for writing poems.

Suitable for

KS2

Aims

- To develop the ability to select precise words.
- To develop a critical appreciation of language.
- To write in a specific poetic form.

Resources

- A selection of poetry books
- Dictionaries

What to do

Acrostic Poems

1. Share examples of acrostic poems with the class. The title of the poem is written vertically and forms the initial letter of each line.

2. Write some acrostics together. Take a title and brainstorm what it suggests.

3. Select the key messages and write each line of the acrostic poem. Look at example for 'football' on page 362.

Fiercely defending the goal

Opponents rush towards us

Only to be stopped by a stunning save

Team spirit is high

Balls pierce the damp air

Attack is all

Leading to a win

Loving the success!

4. The children can then write their own acrostic poems. Using a dictionary can help them with the initial words in each line.

Limericks

1. Explain that limericks are short amusing poems of five lines that follow a particular pattern.
   - The first line introduces the character.
   - The second and first lines rhyme with the fifth line.
   - The third and fourth shorter lines rhyme with each other.

2. Share some limericks with the children. Edward Lear wrote many in his *The Book of Nonsense* in 1846. Here are just a couple.

   There was an Old Man with a beard,
   Who said, 'It is just as I feared!
   Two Owls and a Hen,
   Four Larks and a Wren,
   Have all built their nests in my beard!'

   There was a Young Lady whose chin,
   Resembled the point of a pin;
   So she had it made sharp,
   And purchased a harp,
   And played several tunes with her chin.

3. Model how to create a limerick.

4. Have a set of name lists handy for the first line as they can help the children to get started.

5. Brainstorm words that rhyme with the name and which help with the first, second and fifth lines.

6. Add the rhyming couplet for lines three and four.

7. Ensure that there is a theme to the verse.

8. Ask the children to work in pairs or groups to create their own limericks. A class book of limericks can be produced which can be illustrated.

Questions and Answers

Work with the whole class collaboratively or in small groups to hone writing skills. The aim is to write and answer questions that can be collated into a collaborative or individual poem. Note that, for Key Stage 1, this process will need to be modelled first, working together to produce a class collection of questions and answers, then sending the children off to work in pairs or small groups.

Suitable for

KS1, KS2

Aims

- To encourage experimentation with language.
- To focus on vocabulary.
- To write with precision and effect.

Resources

- Collection of poems that pose questions
- A box
- Prompt cards (see page 365)

What to do

1. Read the poems to the children.
2. Remind them of the question words – who, what, when, why, where and how.
3. Ask them to write a question. They do not need to know the answer – indeed, they should think of a broad question that may have no definitive answer.
4. Put the questions into the box.

5. Ask each child to pick a question from the box and answer it – writing only one line initially. It may be helpful for the children to work in pairs at this point. The aim is for them to write an unusual and imaginative answer. Here are some examples of questions and answers.

- *Question* How far can a swallow swoop?
- *Answer* To the bottom of the deepest pit.

- *Question* Where do the acorns fall?
- *Answer* Beneath the mud of the ancient riverbank.

- *Question* When does the Moon disappear?
- *Answer* When the clouds stretch to space and beyond.

6. Each child then reads out their question and corresponding answer.

7. A collaborative poem can be created from the responses, as a whole class or in groups. This will necessitate re-reading and developing an awareness of the rhythm of each line.

Suggestions for prompt cards

Having lists of nouns and prepositions can be helpful prompts when you introduce this activity. Here are some examples:

Common nouns

The world of nature and science can be a good starting point: Sun, Moon, stars, tree, flower, bush, grass, leaf, Jupiter, Saturn, Neptune, sea, rocks, beach, cave, clouds, rain, fog, grass, electricity, magnet.

Prepositions

Above, across, after, against, around, beneath, beside, below, between, by, during, inside, in front of, near, on, opposite, past, towards, underneath, within.

Variation

- Ask questions relating to a specific theme, such as space, the weather, journeys and so on.

Behind the Door

This activity generates some unusual images, which help to stimulate imaginative writing.

Suitable for

KS1, KS2

Aims

- To develop the imagination.
- To play with language.
- To create a shared poem.

Resources

- Prompt cards, one colour for common nouns, another for abstract nouns (see page 367)

What to do

1. Introduce the starter sentence 'Behind the door I found ... .'
2. Pick up two cards – one common and one abstract noun, such as *glass* and *peace*.
3. Create a sentence linking the two words – in this case, 'Behind the door I found a *glass* of *peace*.'
4. Turn over further cards to create more unusual images and add them to the list.
   - Behind the door I found a *ship* of *trust*.
   - Behind the door I found a *spoon* of *weakness*.
   - Behind the door I found a *thimble* of *joy*.
   - Behind the door I found a *chest* of *compassion*.
5. Collate these lines to form a shared poem.

Examples of common and abstract nouns

Common nouns

Armchair, bag, boat, bowl, box, briefcase, building, chair, chest, cupboard, garage, house, jar, plane, sofa, spoon, suitcase, table, vase, wardrobe.

Abstract nouns

Amazement, anger, anxiety, beauty, deceit, enthusiasm, fear, generosity, grace, humour, pain, peace, romance, sadness, warmth, weakness, wit, worry.

Variations

- Use other introductory lines, such as the following:
  - Once upon a time, there was ...
  - Over the rainbow you'll find ...
  - The other day she noticed ...
- Take one line of the 'Behind the door' poem and use it as the title for a poem on that theme. So, for example, for 'Behind the door I found a **thimble of joy**', '**Thimble of joy**' becomes the title of another poem.

Non-fiction activities

Walk the Talk!

Children often find it quite difficult to write non-fiction texts. Each text type has its own structure and language features and it can take children a long time to get to grips with these. Sue Palmer uses a 'Two horses before the cart' model to explain what's required. The first horse stands for learning about the curriculum content and how to organise this content for writing. The other horse stands for reading lots of examples of the text type and being given plenty of practice in 'talking' the text type. Both horses are needed to 'pull the cart' – that is, before children can progress and write their own non-fiction texts. To this end, writing frames can be extremely useful, helping children to organise the content of their writing.

Suitable for

KS1, KS2

Aims

- To make explicit links between reading and writing.
- To support children in organising non-fiction writing.

Resources

- Writing frames and prompts (various)
- Mini-whiteboards and pens

What to do

1. Model how to use the writing frames before giving them to the children. This is particularly important for *young* children.
2. There are many writing frames available, including Sue Palmer's Skeleton Frames. See the examples on page 371.

Simple report frame for a non-chronological report, KS1

What is it?

What does it look like?

Where is it found?

What is it used for?

Report frame for a non-chronological report, KS2

Report

Title _____

Introduction
I have been finding out about _____
_____
_____

I have learned that _____
_____
_____

I have learned that _____
_____
_____

Simple explanation frame, KS1

M I want to explain how I _____
y _____
_____
_____
_____

e
x First I _____
p _____
l _____
_____

a Then it _____
n _____
a _____
t _____

i This is because _____
o _____
n _____
_____
_____

Further sources of information

- For activities linked to reading non-fiction texts, see Persuade Me! (page 196) and This is What you Do (page 183). For ideas linked to 'talking' the text type, see Telling My News (see **www.pearsoned.co.uk/glynne**) and Talk Prompts for Explanation and Discussion, page 22.
- Sue Palmer, *How to Teach Writing across the Curriculum at Key Stage 1* (David Fulton, 2003) and *How to Teach Writing Across the Curriculum at Key Stage 2* (David Fulton, 2001).

Did You Know?

This activity provides a structure for presenting simple facts linked to work on information texts. It is a very good activity to use with any information topic and provides a strong link between reading and writing. It shows children how to write a simple fact with some additional information in a clear way.

Suitable for

KS1

Aims

- To make explicit links between reading and writing.
- To support information writing.

Resources

- Simple information texts
- Writing frame – 'Did You Know?'

What to do

1. Choose an information book that you have looked at with the children during shared reading. Focus on a page and pick out one piece of information. Explain why you have chosen that fact and then model how to write the information in a 'Did You Know?' box. Write two sentences – the first stating the fact, the second giving some extra information, such as on page 374.

2. Ask the children to talk to their partners about a key fact that they have learned from the topic. They can then work in pairs and write their own 'Did You Know?' boxes. Alternatively, each pair can be given a simple information book and be asked to locate an important fact to write in their box.

Example of a 'Did You Know? box

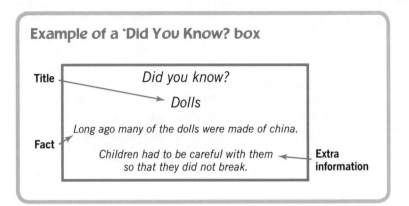

Fact file

Young children find it hard to write key facts they have found in information texts. We talk with them about writing things 'in their own words' but often they just copy sentences from the book they have read. This activity provides a structure to help children organise and present simple facts. It can be used to support children's work once they are familiar with 'Did you Know?' boxes (see page 374).

Suitable for

KS1, could be adapted for KS2 – see page 377

Aims

- To make explicit links between reading and writing.
- To support information writing.

Resources

- Simple information texts
- Fact file writing frame from page 376 (enlarged version for modelling process – this could be on an interactive whiteboard and A4 versions for the children) (See **www.pearsoned.co.uk/glynne**)
- Flipchart or whiteboard

What to do

1. Revisit an information book that you have read with the children. Read one of the pages and model how to pick out some of the key facts. Write them on a flipchart or whiteboard. (If you are using an electronic or multimodal text you could underline the facts in different colours to make the process clearer to the children.)

2. Read another page to the children and ask them to talk with their partner to see if they can pick out two important facts. Repeat this process for one or two more pages and then move on to modelling how to use the writing frame.

3. Look at the facts you have gathered with the children. Talk about how some of the facts could link together. For example, in the topic 'Homes in the past – Castles' you could have gathered facts about the different parts of the castle and the rooms. Demonstrate to the children how the facts could be grouped together before modelling how to write the facts.

4. The children could then work in pairs (each pair using different books but on the same topic) to locate key facts, which can then be used for their own fact file. Some pairs could locate facts on a website although this is a more difficult skill.

5. Once the children have completed their fact files they could be shared with another pair or group of children. Have they found any different information? Are some books/websites easier to use than others?

Example fact file

Castle Fact File

Keep

Picture

Moat

Ramparts

Battlements

Great Hall

Variation

- This approach can be adapted for KS2 to support children in using more than one source. Children could locate key facts from two or three books/websites and then produce a fact file in booklet form.

Activities to Support Non-chronological Reports

These two activities use oral rehearsal to prepare children for writing non-chronological reports by encouraging them to look closely at objects and pick out key features.

Suitable for

KS1

Aims

- To make explicit links between speaking, listening and writing.
- To begin to write simple non-chronological reports.

Resources

- Writing frames for Similarities and Differences (see page 379)
- Paper and pencils

What to do

Similarities and Differences

1. Ask the children to compare two objects (or two animals). They could look for one or two things that are similar or different. Initially, ask them to do an oral comparison to help them organise their thoughts. Later, they can draw the objects and complete a simple writing frame, such as the example on page 379.

Example of a writing frame for Similarities and Differences

Similarities and Differences

I have looked at a .... and a ....

I have found one thing that is similar.

....

I have found one thing that is different.

....

What to do

Tell Me Maps

1. This is a simple frame to support the children's descriptions of an object. It can be used as a link between oral and written work.

2. Initially, model how to produce a Tell Me Map so that the children understand how to use the frame. In a whole-class session, draw a simple outline of an object linked to a current topic, such as a dinosaur. Talk with the children about the key features of the object or they could discuss these with a partner. Model how to label the outline with the key features – what it looks like, where it lives and what it eats, for example.

3. Next, the children work with a partner to produce their own Tell Me Maps. They can then use these to give oral descriptions of their object. In a later session, the frame could be used to help them produce a simple written report.

What it looks like.

Where it lives.

What it eats.

The Cheese Sandwich

It is important for children to be able to organise key aspects of information when writing non-fiction texts. This graphic organiser can help children arrange their ideas before writing them.

Suitable for

KS2

Aims

- To make explicit links between reading and writing.
- To organise relevant information for writing non-fiction texts.

Resources

- Cheese Sandwich frames (see page 381)

What to do

1. Before using this graphic organiser, the children will need a great deal of practice in identifying the main ideas and supporting details in texts (such as Get the Idea, page 126).

2. Modelling how to use the Cheese Sandwich frame is very helpful, so the children understand its purpose.

3. Choose an aspect of a particular topic, for example, from history or geography. Remind the children about the concepts of a main idea and supporting details, then demonstrate how to make notes using the frame (see page 381).

4. Then the children work in pairs or individually, using the frame to help them organise their notes about another aspect of the topic. The completed frames then provide the bare bones for their more detailed pieces of writing at a later stage.

Cheese Sandwich frame

Write your topic at the top. Add details to the middle layers. Add a concluding sentence at the bottom.

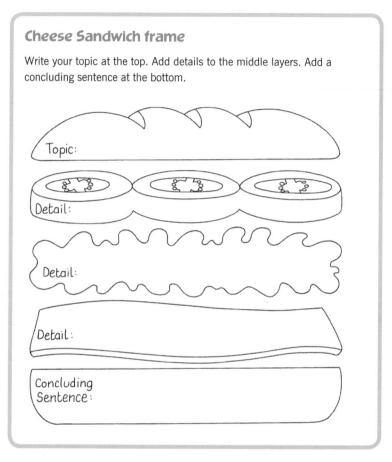

Topic:

Detail:

Detail:

Detail:

Concluding Sentence:

Additional materials to support this activity can be viewed/downloaded at
www.pearsoned.co.uk/glynne

In the News

Producing a class or school newspaper gives the children a real audience for their writing.

Suitable for

KS2

Aims

- To write for a real audience.
- To write in a range of genres.

Resources

- Selection of newspapers
- Digital camera (optional)

What to do

1. Decide whether your newspaper will be produced electronically or in paper format.
2. Share a selection of newspapers with the class. This could include newspapers that are aimed at children, such as *First News* or *The Newspaper*.
3. Review the layout and range of subjects covered in different types of newspapers.
4. Decide on the audience for your newspaper:
   - other children in the school
   - parents
   - the local community.
5. Consider the extent of the distribution of the finished product. Will several copies be produced or just one for the class?

6. Divide the children into groups. Allocate each group a subject area, then let the children choose which aspect of those subjects they wish to work on. Here are some possible subject areas:

- news
- features
- sport, including match reports
- fashion
- book, film, music reviews
- clubs
- events, such as a school fair, quizzes, book week and so on
- outing reports
- competition
- letters page
- interviews – with visitors to the school, parents, staff.

7. Ensure the children plan their questions before any interviews. You could even help them send a list to an interviewee by e-mail prior to a face-to-face meeting. Alternatively, they could ask several people the same question, such as 'Is school uniform a good idea and, if so, why?', and write an article based on their responses.

8. Revise the key elements of report writing:

- use the present tense
- use the third person
- the who, what, why, when, where and how must be included in the first paragraph
- use the inverted triangle for news reports – that is, most important information first, followed by successively less important details.

9. The groups work on their writing in pairs or individually.

10. If using a digital camera, provide photographs for the newspaper.

11. The children can write their pieces.

12. When they have finished, show them how to proofread and edit their stories.

13. Design headlines.

14. Consider whether or not the newspaper should have a strapline – a phrase that states what the publication is about, such as **Oak Tree News**. *The latest at your local school.*

15. Publish the newspaper and distribute it.

Further sources of information

- www.thenewspaper.org.uk
- www.firstnews.co.uk/teachers
- www.headliners.org
- Suzy Bender, *Just Like a Journalist* (Russell House Publishing, 2009)

Useful websites

General Literacy websites

www.literacytrust.org.uk This organisation provides a wealth of information relating to schools, teaching and literacy (e.g. news, research, events and resources).

www.clpe.co.uk An educational centre for schools, parents and teachers with an international reputation for its work in language, literacy and assessment.

www.ncll.org.uk The National Centre for Language and Literacy is based at the University of Reading. It runs a range of courses for teachers, has a wealth of resources and participates in research.

www.playbackschools.org.uk/ This website helps you to access the videos from Teachers TV which support primary practice.

www.bbc.co.uk/learning Learning resources for teachers, parents and children.

https://shop.channel4learning.com/ Channel 4 learning resources for teachers and the interactive resource 'Bookbox' which features a range of activities linked to reading and writing.

http://terry-eng42.blogspot.co.uk/ (Previously Learnanytime) This site provides links to many other useful and varied websites providing a variety of literacy resources.

http://www.coxhoe.durham.sch.uk/curriculum/Literacy.htm This is an excellent school website which provides links to a range of interactive activities.

Speaking and Listening (including Drama)

www.sfs.org.uk Storytellers Society website, which provides a wealth of information about storytelling.

www.storymuseum.org.uk/1001stories/ This website provides an opportunity to read and listen to a variety of stories for all ages from around the world.

www.rsc.org.uk/education/ Royal Shakespeare Company's education department.

http://www.artsonthemove.co.uk/ This site has some useful information about drama methods and games.

http://www.dramaresource.com/ An excellent site that provides information about drama techniques and games.

http://www.moeplanning.co.uk/category/planning/ Information and ideas to support the 'Mantle of the Expert' technique.

http://www.bigeyedowl.co.uk/roleplay.htm and

http://www.nurseryactivityideas.co.uk/category/role-play-activities (Both these sites have useful ideas for role play).

Reading

http://www.booktrust.org.uk/books-and-reading/children/ A comprehensive website which encourages reading for all ages and provides a range of information and resources.

http://fileserver.booktrust.org.uk/usr/resources/239/looking-at-books-the-big-picture-guide-to-exploring-picture-books.pdf Resources for looking at picture books.

http://www.salfordcommunityleisure.co.uk/sites/default/files/uploads/documents/Schools%20weblinks%202012.pdf A booklet produced by Salford School's Library Service containing a list of web addresses for publishers, authors and other book-related websites.

www.firstnews.co.uk/teachers/free-resources Children's newspaper.

www.headliners.org National news agency for young people aged 8–18 years.

Film

http://old.bfi.org.uk/education/teaching/primary.html British Film Institute's excellent moving image resources.

http://www.filmeducation.org This site provides a wide range of resources linked to a variety of films.

Writing (including Poetry)

http://www.poetryarchive.org/childrensarchive/poemsHome.do Poems performed by poets online.

www.poetrysociety.org.uk/ Provides development opportunities for poets, teachers and pupils.

www.applesandsnakes.org Performance poetry organisation: poets, events and educational resources.

Grammar

http://www.childrensuniversity.manchester.ac.uk/interactives/languages/words/ Some useful interactive support for nouns and adjectives.

Spelling

http://www.amblesideprimary.com/ambleweb/lookcover/lookcover.html An online activity using the Look, Cover, Write, Check approach. You can use the ready-made lists or input your own.